Frances Presley
Collected Poems Volume 1

ALSO BY FRANCES PRESLEY

The Sex of Art
Hula-Hoop
Linocut
Neither the One nor the Other, *with Elizabeth James*
Automatic Cross Stitch, *with Irma Irsara*
Somerset Letters
Paravane
Myne
Lines of Sight
Stone settings, *with Tilla Brading*
An Alphabet for Alina, *with Peterjon Skelt*
Halse for Hazel
Sallow
Ada Unseen
ADADA, *with Tilla Brading*
Collected Poems Vol. 2

Frances Presley

Collected Poems

Volume 1
1973–2004

Shearsman Books

First published in the United Kingdom in 2022 by
Shearsman Books Ltd
PO Box 4239
Swindon
SN3 9FN

Shearsman Books Ltd Registered Office
30–31 St. James Place, Mangotsfield, Bristol BS16 9JB
(this address not for correspondence)

ISBN 978-1-84861-811-4

Copyright © Frances Presley, 1973–2022

The right of Frances Presley to be identified as the author of this work has been asserted by him in accordance with the Copyrights, Designs and Patents Act of 1988. All rights reserved.

Acknowledgements
We are grateful to Salt Publishing for permission to reproduce work from the author's *Paravane: new and selected poems 1996–2003* (Cambridge: Salt Publishing, 2004).

Contents

The Sex of Art
1973–86

America
Pennsylvania wilderness	17
Birmingham, Alabama	18
After Washington	19
Spiralling out of Maine	20
Newsmen	21
Another Failed Futurist Poem	22

Heroes of our time
The One	25
The shooting of Pechorin	26
"Fixed on the wall…"	27
Carnal knowledge	28
"Style is excused by fever…"	29
"Too blatant for deceit…"	30
Portrait of a Writer	31
4 a.m. Ditchling Rise	33
The Ezra Pound papers	34

The Right Balance
Le juste milieu	39
North Face	43
From the Jura	44
The Contemporary Poet in Paris	45

Germany in Autumn
Anniversary poem	49
Autumn now	52
Letters to Heidelberg	54
Love poem	59
Free Union	60

The Community Project

The community project	65
Highgate Cemetery	66
Deconstruction	67
Sari	68
Orgreave	69
Greeks	70
British Museum	71
Uscita	72
Eight dead as gang fires on Naples crowd	73
Reconstruction	74

The Sex of Art

Niki St. Phalle	77
Tinguely	78
Gwen John	79
The Dinner Party	80

Holland: Ithaca

Holland : Ithaca	85
Ithaca : The Haven	86

Hula Hoop
1986–1989

Inside Britannia

Keeping safe	91
Relaxation routine	93
The Common Good	95
Natural reaction	96
Equal Opportunities 3	98
Black 1	100
Community charge	101
Integrity at Christmas	102

Hula Hoop
    Hula hoop   105
    Summer holiday   107
    Boat train   108

Community art
    The sculptor   111
    The giant at Queen Victoria School   113
    Carnival   115
    Linear construction   116
    The Shelter Sketchbook 1941   117
    Miró   118
    for virginia firnberg   119
    Deadlier than the Male Cabaret, Cardiff   120

Linocut
1989–1995

Linocut   125
Solar in Paris   126
Leonora at the Serpentine   129
Imago   130
Masks   131
A girl and her shadow   132
Magia di siepi montanari   133
Two trees for Georgia O'Keeffe   134
Swan songs   135
MAD?   137
The second collage   138
The dream   140
Stasis   141
Saint Malo   144
Rimbaud in Cheltenham   146
anglia   147
Coal   148
Significant moments in the life of my mother   150
Leitrim Observer   151

Wightlink	153
Pilgrims' Way	154
New Forest, August 1990	155
Purple, white & green	156
The Nunnery Walks	157
Miscarriage	158
Hair washing in the country	161
The souffleur	162
This March	164
Statement	165

Automatic cross stitch
1995–96
by Frances Presley and Irma Irsara

PIECE WORK: A WALK AROUND THE FASHION INDUSTRY

piece work/the sound of the sewing machine	171
bangla	172
stitching	173
overlocking	176
the factory owner	177
the machinists	179
Fonthill Road fashion shops	
looking	180
the importance of sizing	181
Dream designs	182
Vogue	183
warehouse	185

WRITE THE DRESS

white gloves	189
buttons	190
the girl's dress	192
mini	194
crushed velvet x 2	
black crushed velvet	195
yellow crushed velvet	196

    fetish   197
    Veronicas   200
    Mary Wollstonecraft in outer costume   202

Images

    coat hangers   175
    rose linear   199
    bobbins   203
    sewing machine   204

Notes   205

Private writings:
Vermont journal, September 1996   207
with drawings by Peterjon Skelt

Neither the One Nor the Other   223
1998–99
by elizabeth james and Frances Presley

Somerset letters
1993–2001
with drawings by Ian Robinson

Letter 1   243
The Iris   245
Hollow ways   246
Letter 2   247
Dry fur   249
Park range   250
Letter 3   251
Letter 4   252
A brief history of Somerset   254
Minehead   255

Seeing oaks	257
Coleridge notebook	258
Letter 5	260
Letter 6	263
Letter 7	263
Letter 8	264
Blurred passage	265
Blithedale postcard	268
Mineheads	270
Letter 9	271
Letter 10	272
Somerset letters : note	274

Paravane
9/11/2001–11/9/2002

Paravane day	277
Ground O	278
Underwriters	280
9/2	282
Stonenest street	285
11/9	286
Fluid Canvas	288
Subject: Re: Semtex	290
Post scriptorum	292
Garrigill (1 Nov)	295
Stonenest street (1 Jan 02)	296
Garrigill (23 May)	297
Black burn	298
Tertia at St Mary Magdalene	299
Othery cope	300
Julian of Norwich	
Her cell	302
for Joan Brossa	303
first flame	304
Notes	306

Uncollect
1998–2004

Conductor	309
The Landscape Room	311
Huboub	314
A comedy for Colette	316
Windcorner	318

Myne
2003–2004

March: on North Hill	325
in St Michael's	327
April: from Greenaleigh to Porlock Bay	328
June: on North Hill	330
October: on North Hill	332
November: in St Michael's	334
December: in St Peter's	335
February: in St Michael's	337
March: on North Hill	339
in St Michael's	340
in St Peter's	341
April: on Grabbist	342

Acknowledgements	345

THE SEX OF ART

1973–86

America

Pennsylvania Wilderness

Coming down to the Susquehanna
through the burnished gaming forests
of late Fall
I saw youth
with an outdated headband
poised in the wind of an outstretched rock
"Are you the new ghost of the Susquehanna?"
I inquired with sly hope

But the smile as his head turned around
was empty
and he asked us only for fresh water

Birmingham, Alabama

Three days of paranoia
a loaded gun always at hand
I lay against the crinkled grass
of a Jewish grave
because the black neighbourhood
was forbidden
The state of siege is alleviated
when my aunt allows me out to the library

Where
a host of multicoloured children
gabble like Thanksgiving turkeys at story time
or flap their wings
like fabled eagles together

After Washington

Though the nuns have fallen asleep
beneath the white mist wraps
as the bus slowly creeps to Pennsylvania
my eyes are still open
to a crumbling city
the startled eyes of a black worker
flagging down our bus with orange flag
for the emergency cement mixers filling
in surreptitious holes

Somewhere in the centre of the insectlights
is the one who issues confused officials.
(in the station)
"Show me your ticket"
"Hey man, what do you think I am
some kind of bum?
you sick or something?"
"I'm only doing my job"
"Why don't you search them?"

Gesture to the whites
a nun stirs uneasily in sleep
the black bible slides to her feet

Spiralling out of Maine

White angles razor
a fish back kicked
numbed by Ogunquit sands
'a permanent condition'
Sucked by uneven prints
the sea fragmented
our shells
splashed down
an inert brown jellyfish
or a broken lobster claw
rasping attention
at the net of an unlicensed
fisherman

In Maine
there was a clam
thrown loose to the reality
of flotsam
and now bubbles blind flesh
in its tight shell

Newsmen

Yes WGAL 8 newsmen
cry
They do their job
They sit in their bathtubs
think about the bloody waters
and cry
They watch governments shake
tremble over their buttered toast
and cry

We are human they assure us
even if we're not allowed
to tell you about it.

Another Failed Futurist Poem

Number 964409
has tested out the John F Kennedy space center
and castigated the applied engineers
for not assembling more thunderstorms
Despite Von Braun's welcome
and the star trekked campaign of our founder
the tapes have ten years' static
Where is my five second main boost?

Now the military
plagiarise their minute men and honest johns
A skeletal staff
gloom around the space shuttle

It may carve thru the open window
to Soyuz next July
but they're having doubts about the Soviets
"They've given us a bad link up time
They're taking our ideas
Let's get back to Cape Canaveral
and quit fixing Von Braun's electric shaver"

The coaches at NASA
are for our older Greyhound drivers
Observe the museums
of previous construction space
We're all stopping
to take account
    and playback.

Heroes of Our Time

The One

Young men's poems
delve their sad memories into the earth
for a fecund promise
that always slides moist from their fingers

Perhaps if they took the soil itself?
and so to leaning back beneath the loam of suffocation
splaying out limbs
in hope of becoming supine clay
themselves a prostrate though muscle-bound
angel

The pictures of Caravaggio
with their creamtinted othereyed saviours
holding regular arms in commissioned framework
while beard tormented snubnosed saint Francis
collapses
on the cushioned support of his favourite boy

and do I have pity
when one whimpers for its other?

Look how it can watch and twist itself
lock and indifferently wither its sinews
be saint Jerome
use only the bone needed to carve a word
in the light of a skull

and do I
now we are one?

The Shooting of Pechorin
for A.P.

Steady yourself at the rock edge
there, where your foot fits against the stone
and blades of complicit grass
clasp tight around your heel
you can be steady
you know it is a lie brings you here
my love, you are thinking of the wrong lie
leave it there
for now no shifts of soil
will dare dislodge beneath you
nor impact of fire push you
back
yours is the balance
because you know you know yourself

"Fixed on the wall…"

Fixed on the wall
with no apparent strings
the face of Christ
eyes averted from the light

or else he might see across the room
the Virgin Mary who croons
to a child's head
through soundless lips

On the white walls
no other adornment

Below perhaps a blanket fold
pink or purple

Two hands lock in silence
between unavoided eyes

Carnal Knowledge

It ceased to give pleasure
the concave body which made full
became thin
Even the scooping gesture
became blunted and dull

So they held up instead
the poem above their heads
which signalled the transparence of one
for the other a moment to be gone

"This woman is reduced to a line
perhaps not even implied
What do we know of her?
Something of an intellectual bore?"

He did allow a gesture of analysis
for his seed was irretrievable
a cloud-rift of 'there might have been'
an adjunct to the morning-after kiss

"Style is excused by fever…"

Style is excused by fever
dilated beneath the eyes
of the boy whose thin veins
ran blue through your page forever

Later we know he walked away
through swung hotel doors
down imploring corridors
We know you turned your hands away
to the iron frame that became a bed
where twisted arms climb
and attendants recognise no signs
at a crossed frontier

That limpid boy
was employment for only a page
which created itself
See, it is the face of your white self

"Too blatant for deceit..."

Too blatant for deceit
you would turn your back cloth side to me
and hang its silk lining black
before my eyes
and retract all talk of the heart
for to talk of that
dare I say is also your part

In our 'communal' bath
you would lie immersed for hours
while I snatched a towel
fearing not to dry myself

"You do not think" you said
"really about death as I do
Pass me the shampoo"

Portrait of a writer

"He wrote for women, always for women. If he gave a poem or a story to a particular woman it was rarely the woman who had initially inspired him. Yet he always had the impression that the text belonged to her, that she had become the true owner of a certain poem or story."

In this way, his self-criticism began. A game of mirrors which created the desired effect and left me dazzled. Self-criticism, because under the pretext of writing a biography, playing the role of objective critic and quoting from an author's private unpublished diaries, he was evidently writing the story of his own life.

Most of the extracts taken from the diary concern a young girl, the writer's first love, whose Christian name we are told, but whose surname is pure fiction: 'Linda Musen'. Linda of the blond hair, cut in the nape of the neck in a style too simple not to have been expensive; Linda who wore the olive green coat; Linda, whom our author, lack of experience perhaps, failed to keep in his real life.

After watching her leave for the last time he undergoes a night of crisis, signalled in the diary by a series of metaphors which so greatly impressed the 'critic'. He points to them as evidence of the growth of an author who must rid himself of this heap of images.

These metaphors had, as their source, the name Muse, and I remember some of them: the letter M written on his forehead, M of morphine engraved on his forehead by this woman, and, at the end, he cries: 'Dreadful Muse, will I never be rid of you'.

To be faithful to the text, I should add that the critic tells us the author survived this period of despair, partly due to more successful sexual relationships. Unfairly I could add a third mirror by saying that this second stage of the author's life – that of emotional tranquillity – did not take place. Perhaps I don't have the right, but in all fairness, this portrait is only a fiction…

As a writer, then, I accuse you and will not let you be a complacent critic. This mark 'M', sign of misery and with reason! You remember the title of the film, made by that great director Fritz Lang, which was written in chalk on the murderer's back, unknown to him. It is the sign inscribed in the hollow of everyone's hand, but which our writer succeeds in planting on someone else's forehead and, simultaneously, sticking it to his own. A murderer who projects not a metaphor, this much abused word, but a symbol which shapes another, destroys another, and then the murderer feels destroyed by the reflection of his own work. This is the fundamental distinction between the metaphor and the symbol.

As I myself have assumed the role of second critic I am going to complete the history of our story 'Alfred and the Muses'. Alfred Pleasant was the pseudonym our writer chose: he wished at all costs to remain anonymous, only revealing a fragment of his game. It was indeed a competition that was at stake – a short story competition for which a small prize had been proposed. 'Alfred' won. The judge, a man of letters, himself a novelist, though little known owing to his obscure modern style, was doubtless attracted by the double game of characters. Perhaps he had even recognised a certain resemblance to his own state of mind. I suggest the possibility, I don't know for sure.

It only remains for me to mention the woman, owner for some time of the short story – one of Linda's successors. She revealed the author's name to a friend who was responsible for the competition. The latter, sending back the original manuscript to 'Alfred Pleasant' implied her knowledge of the pseudonym. The writer, laid bare, never forgave her and it was the last text she ever received from him.

Written from memory in French and translated.

4 a.m. Ditchling Rise

– A red brick wall
teeth on edge
a finger chimney
and our bed –
"Is this *simple* enough?
my dream asked

You laughed
brown head vibrating
with the first train
on the stained pillow
Cup your hand against my forehead
A cure for The Railway's
whisky throb
our temples pulse
with the blackened viaduct
where the train winds
and my finger slides
round your eyelid

Last night the landlord wiped a glass
watched our whisky kiss, you said
"He thinks I'm doing the decent thing by you
but THE SPIRIT OF THE RAILWAY WORKER IS NOT DEAD"
chalk letters on a siding shed.

The Ezra Pound Papers

There was Tom, a 'naively enthusiastic' Canadian, on his own admission. He had once met Olga Rudge when she was in Canada: she had apparently been interested in his deep blue eyes (and perhaps his logger's physique). Tom required no more than this intimation of interest. She suggested he come over and be a working guest in Marie de Rachewiltz's castle. Thus Tom was to meet not only Ezra Pound's mistress but also his daughter. A few weeks later he sent a telegram signed 'Blue Eyes' and went. At the end of his long and tortuous journey he saw, standing at the castle entrance, dressed in white gauze which seemed to float in the dim evening light, Patricia. She was the most beautiful girl he had ever seen, and the fact that she was Pound's grand-daughter only enhanced that beauty.

He was also able to meet Olga Rudge again in Venice. She rarely receives visitors. He sent a note up to her apartment saying that he would be in Chico's around the corner, if she wanted to see him. He knew that Chico's had been a favourite meeting place for Olga and Ezra. She sent a note of invitation and the first thing Tom did on entering her room was to stroke the stone head of E.P which Gaudier-Brzeska had carved and which Olga Rudge now possesses.

Tom was only one of a group of academics who came to a conference on this American poet, held at Keele University last year. There were only two 'non-professionals': one was an engineer and the other a psychiatrist who worked in Washington D.C. – someone said he looked a bit like Erlichmann, one of the Nixon gang. He was smooth, yes. Skin that was puffed and iced, small features, hair that wisped to the right. He looked at you steadily, mildly. He was not a relative collector, but when young had known the man himself. Pound was at that time an inmate of St. Elizabeth's asylum in Washington.

"I was able to talk to him then because I believed in his politics. I knew nothing about his poetry until later. He would only talk politics with his visitors, you know. Only once did I, personally, see him get angry with a visitor. It was when a woman brought her Jewish friend without first asking. He didn't tell her to get out, exactly, but…

Ezra used to take his women visitors behind the bushes, you know… He was an immensely strong man then. I played tennis with him, too." The psychiatrist made a sweeping gesture with his arm to imitate the strength of the literary lion. "He declined so quickly after he left. You've seen the pictures of him. He suddenly became an old man."

"There were those," I said, "who thought it would have been better for him to stay there."

"Oh. I don't know. He so much wanted to leave…"

"Yes. I know; but when he did leave he collapsed into senility. Perhaps it was a little like the London years. He needed people around him in order to produce his best work, even those he hated most."

"Yes, he was surrounded by people. You may be right." He suddenly laughed and became excited. "But he dropped us all after he left. Even C. who had spent three years in jail for him. Three years in jail. He just came out and told C. that he couldn't see him anymore. He had been told to drop his connection with C. if he wanted to get out. So he did."

The man who said perhaps the most to me was another Canadian. Each time I saw him I found it impossible to remember the physical details of his appearance, yet his words, about the lecture he was going to deliver stayed in my mind. At first I had not understood him. I said, referring to the imminent lecture: "You can get it published, I suppose."

"No. Charlie Terrell will think it too critical." Charlie Terrell is the editor of the official Pound magazine.

"Of Pound, you mean."

"Yes."

"Oh."

Now the lines concentrated towards him. The room was dark. The rain riveted down upon the Midlands, the flat lands, the home lands. Terrell was chairman then, upright in his chair, arms folded, the stiff, unhappy general of an army about to be defeated. Briefly his army of contributors would be swept aside by the spectres one man raised.

EP SPEECH AGAINST THE PROCESS

Between the morning and the afternoon
between the bright wooden slats of the room
which cradled the caught sounds
of the Provençal lyric
and the dark ceiling timber
which ran towards another speaker
his voice confusing with the rain:

> "This was the man who used a swastika in his letterhead
> who praised his hostess for
> the Aryan character of her guests
> who took Mussolini's weakest jest
> as the greatest sign of intelligence
> If a blind error was committed under Hitler's direction
> it could only occur because he was 'furious from perception'
> who believed like the Führer
> that 'Humanity is malleable mud'"

Ignore the chips from the stone
Any sculptor would

The Right Balance

Le juste milieu

1

If you want silence
if you want a poem
breaking beyond the page
we must not take each others' traces
breaking the ice in the mud
avoiding the brown frost of the lake
for all that the snow can give you
    you already have
a photograph

II

Saint George and the dragon
defunct saint at Bâle cathedral
turns a spear through mouth and tail
You have the photograph now
do not develop it
kneel squint against the sun
for some other red statue
(woman with a lampshade
wearing a carpet)
leave negative the head
in the cold
in the turn of a collar

III

Although rigidity was the accusation
when a thrust of the hand could not make the knee
bend
away from the refusing body
Touch your hips now
Can they yet move or turn?
Look strangely at the hand placed there
From your head it is a stranger's hand

IV

She had known him for a short time. He was French, she was English.

"I would never have thought," she said to him one evening, as they returned from a bistro "that I could speak in French to someone like this."

"Oh yes, it's possible" he assured her and his car travelled quickly through the night. "We must always talk to each other" he said "there must never be a lack of equality, an unequal balance."

He talked to her about the right balance. "It is possible to create 'un juste milieu'." It would exist for them. He taught her to ski and each time she fell he asked:

"Can you manage?" ("Tu t'en sors?")
Afterwards he said "You did well for a beginner".

"Yes. I need about half an hour to get used to it and then I feel all right…"

"It's a question of finding the right balance."

One night she said to him: "You know I have thought of a fine short story in the style of Henry James. There would be a girl, an English girl who meets a Frenchman and who believes him when he talks of the 'juste milieu' which exists between them. She constructs her whole life around that phrase and it has all the significance of a true religion for her. From it emanates subtle, valued connotations which she sustains with all the imagination and sensitivity of which she is capable. And you know all Jamesian heroines are capable of an inexhaustible appreciation. Until one day she hears the young French man use this phrase casually to explain a skiing technique. She suddenly understands, a blinding revelation, that the beautiful phrase was only a cliché."

He smiled "No, it wasn't altogether a cliché."

North Face
for Gerard

If the Alps are grey-shouldered
where are their faces?

Shrunken faces
tight line against the pillow
call it: 'tête reduite'

A slope you can never climb
though you hack one line above another

'But you are blue with fear!' he said

At night the white wax drips
Who has not woken in the early hours
and seen the face of a stranger shining
absorbed in the linen?

When I woke I saw my glasses
upended in the snow beyond my head
and it was not the mountain which bent
to hand them back

From the Jura

Vertical climb of the funiculaire
reading what do I know? philosophy
Cab climbs above the snow line
halfway the rails part
as the two cabs pass
the drivers jump across
one always stays below
the other at Chaumont funi station

Following blue ribbons tied to branches
left for cross country skiers
the ski tracks
my boot marks
on the path between the dark pines
come into a field
low stone wall
on the horizon the 'three chimneys'
Eiger Mönch Jungfrau
below us the flat cantonal fog

Is this the path back?
I run across the field
stop a tractor driver
– Where is Chaumont?
– This is Chaumont
– Yes, but where is the funi?

The Contemporary Poet in Paris
for Yves Bonnefoy

As I unfolded my Michelin Montmartre
it was raining
and street numbers slid me down
the steep cobbles of Rue Lepic
stopped only by an excavator
whose concrete bones lay in square clay holes
I read in *The Times*
that mediaeval gypsum mines
have left the poets' hill a hollow
to be collapsed by new construction.

At the bottom of the slope I found your postwar
apartment and from a baker's shop
I watched its hard grey façade,
wondered which round window was yours
At the entrance a microphone informed me
'M. Bonnefoy is out of the country.'

Germany in Autumn

Anniversary poem

Came into your country
Four sick faces stared from the customs booth
TERRORISTEN !
Fair uniformed young man took unsmiling my passport,
saw my treason.
What use these blown up faces?
(A quoi bon? in French)
Not to help an arrest
but to define the line the patriot treads

In the morning your face blurs
in my eyes, the coarse outline of your head

    Anna didn't like the content of this poem. When I explained to her that this was the anniversary of World War Two, a fact that she, a German was unaware of, although English t.v. had been running historic newsreels in celebration of the event, she insisted that the analogy was entirely false. She is politically leftwing but firmly opposed to the Baader-Meinhof group. Perhaps she disliked the content because it was a celebration of another anniversary: that of my first meeting with the "bear". She found him selfish and calculating. At the time she came to stay he was more interested in Georg Lukács than anyone else. She also knew that he was my main reason for coming to Germany.

    When I arrived at Anna's house her family were all gathered and talking about her love for her East German cousin Peter.
    "To me," said her father, "it is like a love affair during the war. A girl writes to a young soldier in the trenches and it is all very romantic as long as they remain at a distance."
    "How do you know if you will get on together?" asked her sister.
    "Will he be able to find a job here or will he be dependent on you?" asked her mother
    "But really Anna, ten thousand pounds for his release! Can't you find a cheaper man somewhere else?" asked her father.

"You don't have to marry do you?" asked grandmother. "You could just live together at first." She seemed to be satisfied by the idea that a marriage did not have to take place.

Even with my limited knowledge of German I could follow most of their arguments and I had to add "you've never lived with anyone before, Anna."

Peter had married and divorced and Anna said that both of them had tried to forget the existence of the other. Her forgetting had only included brief affairs. I had to admire her romantic desire for unity.

When all the relatives had left I looked around her new place. All her belongings were in a more perfect order. Ordnung. Files, books, tapes, photographs … her large preparation desk, each drawer labelled with the appropriate class number – the class she was teaching at school. I lounged on the sofa, refused most of the food that was offered, and in the days which followed read her beloved Kerouac or went for solitary walks during her teaching hours.

Hundertwasser prints were in the bedroom and perhaps they inspired her to sit up in her sleep at dawn and say "The windows are covered with lollipops." She got up at six a.m. to begin preparation but we sometimes argued after midnight.

"What is your thesis about?" she asked
"Oh I don't know … Surrealism, Abstract Expressionism." I named a few poets and painters including Jackson Pollock.
"I know his work" she said, "he does those things a child of five could do. I've got some reproductions. I'm sure I have." She got out of bed at two a.m. to go and look for them. "What is the value of this?" waving a colour supplement at me. "I could do better."
"It was an expression of inward desires and motivation. An attempt to free them."
"But what use was any of it? Of what importance to anyone else in society?"
"They were committed to social change, they…" I had my doubts too, but she was redirecting my attitudes.

In the morning, drinking something she had provided to improve my health and still arguing…

"It takes five minutes to produce something like that. Where is the skill, the artistry?"

"You're so bourgeois," I exploded and hated myself. I'd vowed never to use that word. She smiled triumphantly and with a deep sense of loss.

Autumn Now
for Anna

I recited Rilke to you or tried to,
as we climbed the path through the vineyard:
the slopes above industrial Esslingen,
where the Gastarbeiter lent on their hoes,
conversed in the sun in another language,
watched us climb
"Twenty per cent of the population is Greek or Turkish"
"Herr es ist Zeit" I persisted,
seeking the climax of a figure disappearing,
erratic molecules combining with the wet descending leaves,
the path awash,
in a rain that won't leave him

And the same night your friends knew the poem and they were political activists. Ro was also a writer and a judge of other people's writing. "So much of what is sent me is so subjective. so personal." I sympathised. Ro's husband came in. He was a socialist politician in local government.

Anna said "You can look for the Rilke here. I'm sure Ro has a copy."

"What was that?" the husband asked. I began to quote "Herr, es ist Zeit" and he finished for me. We found the poem and Ro said "I used to like Rilke very much. You have to admire what he does with the German language. It's really wonderful." She recited a few lines. "But I rejected his ideas when I was sixteen," and she closed the book.

We talked about the lives of artists. She had recently been reading the journals of Thomas Mann. "That is such a dreadful image of the artist" she said "with his precisely ordered, insulated existence" and she gave examples of Mann's daily routine.

Finally I said "My ideal of the artist is not entirely socially responsible. It is of someone like Kerouac, someone living on the edge of society, but who is not shut away from it in a tidy study.

Someone who is poor, who travels and observes. Even Rilke, at least when he lived in a crumbling Parisian hotel room, cannot be entirely condemned."

certain things could be forgiven, accepted,
even the vision of autumn,
"when leaves downrain"

Letters to Heidelberg

When I showed Andreas the 'Anniversary poem' he asked whether I could not perhaps link his name with a patriotic theme instead and, laughing, he added: "I understand poetic licence, but I have to think of my future."

In Heidelberg he was the student prince. His room on the Hauptstrasse was small and bare, but we chose imitation velvet curtains and the colour of the walls was fine. Hauptstrasse now, ringing, jingling bells, the pony cart is fussing past, view of C & A, neat divisions in flag colours, divisions in sweet colours, peaks on red plastic caps. If you look out the back you see flat shadows, landlords saving on expense, saving the family: they do not need to advertise. The Biedermeier portrait of the writer in his garret, huddled in bed, fully clothed, studying, with an umbrella above him to catch the drips from the leaking roof. The modern version of this reads: "'Only poverty produces greatness.' A general truth. Authors demand royalties."

The student prince will show you round the town: "This is where the student prince used to live. It was very squalid. This is where the flood water from the river Neckar came to in 1977 and the student prince had to swim across the street to get his provisions." In the museum you can see portraits of the other student princes, exotically dressed and reclining on silk couches, smoking a pipe perhaps, sword propped against the couch. Perhaps they still live in the fraternity houses exclusively situated on the hillside just where the woods begin.

Today's student prince also knows how to use weapons. He was a soldier.
"What did you do in the army, baby?"
"I resigned once. Or at least I wrote a letter of resignation and left it in the desk drawer where unfortunately the sergeant found it. I was confined to office duties for a week – the worst punishment. I got a certain physical satisfaction out of digging holes for drains,

muscular exhaustion. And," he smiled, "a satisfaction out of the sound that my army boots made when we marched on parade. I was excited then. I was part of something larger than myself. You can't deny it, you can't."

In another modern version there is a photograph of an S.S. gathering in Heidelberg castle during the war, and all the eyes have been carefully masked as if to say that they are alive and well, perhaps in Heidelberg itself and would prefer anonymity.

We sang the folksongs of 1848. They were good songs, written by men fleeing from despotic rulers, rallying the people, all the people with their words, and all the people singing – "Alte wie die Junge" – to do something: "Tun wir etwas dazu." Whether you hammer nails into shoes, or bear a cross, you can help to make one Germany. And so came "Deutschland über alles", itself a product of this enlightened, heroic period. Not a song of domination but of unification. Now we have the songs of Wolf Biermann.

But we never sang Biermann's political songs, only the one which tells of breakfast with Tina. He beat out the rhythm with an egg spoon and then with his feet, bouncing me until the bouncy, laughing rhythm slows into a deep, wordless sexual pause, and then starts again. We ate all the typically German dishes, which he cooked and he would push food into my mouth with his tongue.

In bed he could be an Alsatian dog, pawing me, licking me in a friendly manner, then suddenly barking and snapping ferociously, so that I covered my head and laughed and screamed at him to stop. "Alsatians," he explained, "are often taught to go for the arm of an intruder and not to let go, so if you protect your arm the Alsatian will harmlessly sink his fangs into the protective covering while you drag it round the house looking for something to smash on its head."

"You are someone who is in love with the bear and afraid of him," he said.

In Heidelberg he was Dr. Faustus. He always made someone less confident than himself play God, and snarled out the lines of Faustus' speech:

"Heisse Magister, heisse Doktor gar" ('I am called Master, I am called Doctor'), with all the contempt of an old style actor. He was an intellectual who wrote: "We Germans when we suffer from Weltschmerz must either cry or build systems."

Sometimes he built systems and everything and everyone else ceased to matter. Even the taste of chocolate cake became less important.

We climbed to the Philosophenweg, there you will find the stone inscribed with Hölderlin's famous lines, although there are more popular odes to the city.

"Lange lieb' dich schon, möchte dich, mir zur Lust,
Mutter nennen, und dir schenken ein kunstlos Lied"

1

Where your velvet curtains are
and the green walls rest your mind

there the low mattress
lies easy on the floor

Where the few shelves are
an old pair of plimsolls

Where no heating is
except your body

Where the door is closed and open and

"People commit suicide here too"

you told me

I know

2

In the castle
speak softly
softer than the tourists

Pause in the green glare
which plays on Goethe's exploded tower

Cast your eyes towards the cascade
steps I sat on

Do not forget Neptune
If someone fell from a turret
do not laugh too long

This song was something by Wagner
which you did not recognise
let me hum louder

3

I would have called you mother
or father in this case
but now the leaves are lifted up
and I look up into their thin stirring stomachs
reach for green paint on a roller
soaking the leaf onto the page
as we did at the end of every Nature Walk
except the one which goes through the "Philosophers' Way"

Do you go there alone
Do you see the bum who shuffles
to a cleft in the forest where the water comes down?

Love poem

"Cupid comes with black hair and a moustache"
(Dylan)
The hooks of your charred beard
fall from the yellow skin wax,
thin nostrils ridge your face
you are on hunger strike again
a child who makes a statement
then runs from the family meal
your eyes threaten from the darkest
tunnel wall a wooden train
But when your lips thicken
the creature slips out
and tastes the world,
are caught in my flesh

Free Union

With your hair of wire borrowed from no-man's land
of a forest at the onset of night
of a fakir's bed

with your nose of a cliff ridge
Striding Edge shaking off walkers

with your beard of burnt paper
ever curling away from its own expansion
with your beard that threatens your mouth of cherry liqueur
your mouth of dye water from a Grantham factory

with your back of a bus
moving out into city traffic

with your spine of perfectly spaced steps

with your waist of a beech tree
of a concrete column
of a letter box
of a profaned object
made of cold metal
made of ridged bark

leaning and upright
above the snow floor
above the concrete slabs

with your thoughts at telescopic range

with your fingers of gelignite
with your flannel fingers
in a static blanket
with your fingers of hooks
to suspend their own questions

with your balls of rag dolls
taking in the demand
of every child's hand
with your ripe gooseberry balls
inside a cluster of thorns

with your penis of an old maid
raised by salvation's kiss
the most grateful face I know
with your penis of rock candy
ready to be broken
by the first careless holidaymaker
with your coach tour wheel penis
ready to impress with tarmac facts
your penis a potholer's torch
finding the rock divide

with your eyes
lying at the bottom of a button tin
with your eyes of discarded pebbles
with your eyes
of an unforgiving projector reel
and the dust revolving in its shaft of light

After André Breton's 'L'Union Libre'. A surrealist idea reversed.

The Community Project

The community project

The lower hills are the ones they used
For Sale tacked hugely on the Rochdale mill
My people are a people learning the difference
between detergents and I teach them to use fly killer
See hand, see spray
Their children play in the gutter water smiling
There is no war and the council has constructed metal
elephants for you

He stopped the car just off the motorway, somewhere in the Pennines
and we followed the sheep track with no way down to the river
Looking across the hills his arm bent around me
He said "Shall we go on?" I said no.

Highgate Cemetery

Victorian melodrama is a specialized pleasure
puckering out our smocks in trout fishing days
parsimony hugs the outer lip which is still full
and speaks a perfect message
but the chain now moves from one cog
to the next even forgetting the oil
men conspire to fix brackets on rusty
cemetery gates and
this is the only way I can see rust now.

He notices the 'revolutionary party of Brent
secondary school' and that the Chilean Marxists can't spell.
I notice that the Bangladeshi Marxists
have left their bouquet in its plastic wrapper,
exhalations obscure flowers. Poor Jenny.
No not read never read
Indoctrinated by Edmund Wilson instead.

Sisters of Bethany, three names to each small
metal plaque on a metal stick, a cheap alloy and
I once marked hidden treasure with wooden sticks in
the sand at the vicarage garden fête,
but the Sisters pursue a scorched earth policy, huddled
and bent above the brown grass.

Mary Ann Cross
the cause of Mary Ann hidden
from the main path
This trinity of Mary Ann, George and
the one she called daughter.
No heads, one epigraph.
(Only the daughter talks and talks
dream on Revlon)
But she is dry eyed after the thunderstorm,
after the flood. It is time to visit the doctor's wife.

Deconstruction

I saw you emerge as a rat
in white plaster dust shining
your eyes and nose up towards me

I saw you chew over the joists
suck out the juice from the backbones
and leave a small pile of twigs on the table
which I cleared away

Behind the skirting board you found
a mummified rat
spreadeagled in dessication
only a wind dried duck in the window
of a Chinese restaurant
but grey as a crevice

Later it dangled in the car window
"How could you" I said
as we passed Kew Gardens
"My aunt used to take me to the Chinese pavilion"
you replied
"I asked her why all the steps were broken
and she said that my uncle had done it"

When we came back Rentokil stood
on the doorstep.

It was a warm sunny morning in April.

Sari

I am standing in a chiffon sari
She put me in her petticoat and
her sister's blouse because
I am bigger than her
Then she took the cloth stretched
it out and I held the outstretched cloth
She wrapped it around me making
the three folds or
if you want it tighter make it five
'Tighter it is better for work'
Because the chiffon is all borders
you can refind the pattern
however you fold it
'If you want to be Moslem put
it over your head' and she did
'No, no I do not want to be Moslem'
'Alright.' she said.

You move slowly when you see the straight lines
in the mirror

In the living room
the men
are solving the new maths

Orgreave

"They're running through a corn field
and now through a field of barley"

The miners from the police

Such precision
from our war correspondent!

The precision of journalism which adds
nothing to the story

They are not running from the police
They are running from the precise outline of a black
slag heap or a black mill
above the village rubbish tip
next to the Esso garage

seen through the corn field
(and they were all corn fields)
seen through the poppies
seen through the sunset
seen though the white sticks marking out
the site of the next council estate.

Greeks

On Fonthill Road
male eyes watch to see
if I have a pattern or
am interested in their patterns
Angela Chic
Angel trimmings
Sometimes half seen
are the sewing women
The history of the seamstress survives

One more shirt before dawn

Greek Cypriot that is
Koulla, who married Wayne, our New Zealander
"Koulla. Is that what they call them in New Zealand"
sd Paul who thought it was Kiwi for Sheila
We were glad he didn't take up with an Asian girl
though Koulla's dad made threats
"Why?" asked Wayne
"Because I'm poor bloody Greek that's why."
It took them months to make the sugar roses on the wedding cake
each petal shaped by hand

And I sd "Go downstairs and iron your shirt.
Go on"
"What if I meet someone on the stairs" you sd
"I know. I'll talk about the influence of Greek poetry on the
early Pound"

British Museum

"They always get things wrong
on the exhibition labels"
he said, looking like someone from a housing co-op
We were looking at a gittern
"It can't have been played with a plectrum" he said
"No it can't" you calmly agreed
"But it does say that it was later adapted
to be played as a violin."

I met Chris in a quilted anorak trying
to keep warm amongst the Assyrians.

We had money for the Anglo-Saxon art exhibition
for the gold crosses and brooches

"The cross says: I am drenched and bloody"
They speak to us in runes
"Arthur ordered me to be made"
Tongues of fire glowing out of the manuscript
In the reign of King Cnut

"I think it's a scheme drawn up by Canute to
make the water flow uphill. Lincoln, the worst managed
city in England." Uncle Tom writing from Station Farm.
"We've had a good corn year but the potatoes have no life
in them a good crop ½ out ½ in but we shall survive that's
more than many Ethiopians will."

And they were much preoccupied with Doomsday.

Uscita

We had to leave Venice
because there were no hotels that year
though *Stern* says that there is a new lunatic asylum

Sweets in the streets
but all the signs were completo
Can't take a hotel out of the station
so take a train out the other way
Uscita.

Who are these Italians who want you to get
lost
Uscita.

You came upon me in the train so quickly
Italian stallion saying
– Love. We make love. Amore.
    It is terrible I must go for soldier
– You are young, I say,
    You are twenty and I am thirty
Your fingers search along the base of mine
and do not find the Signora
I say – Say dove. How do you say dove?
Dove long open O
Dove sta memoria, donatello
I say – Your hair is like wire
– Yes, yes, the barbers make it so
Up and up they make it go
My hand bounces off
I say – You are made for love
But I feel your lips like rubber and
my tongue works against yours which works
so hard.

Eight dead as gang fires on Naples crowd

On the streets of Naples
they will sell you paper tissues
fazoletti
and in the cafés
while you eat tagliatelle
or on the bus where
the English woman who married
an Italian said
"My husband is a qualified lawyer but
he can't practice.
You can't be an honest man
and practise law here"
And George said
"Look at those buildings"
"The garden sheds?"
"People live there since the earthquake.
Look at the apartments. Those concrete spans
weren't made to last"
Torn concrete tissues

On the streets of Pompeii
we shared bread rolls called
rosetti
We tore them between our fingers
and wrapped them in tissue.

Reconstruction

Black Périgord
Black Virgin at Rocamadour Roc
    ama
      dour
Blue black curved petal
dragonfly clings to the leaf
Black ants in the coarse grass
The only face she saw that day
was in the uprooted tree

Time to shit and move on
She covered her shit with dead leaves
and a stone
A moment of joy
like the opening scene of Wim Wenders' film
Im Lauf der Zeit
In the run of time
So much better than *Paris-Texas*

Try Chicago-Périgord
And Franklin Collery-Combs
The G.I.'s bastard son who
lost the United States as soon as he was born
I am here to tell you how
ephemeral they are
but also to shake you from all traditions
except your own

"We are now in Mas David, and I work very much on this formidable stone house, and that terrific garden. I was houseman, I am slave, or house-slave. But a happy one!"

The Sex of Art

Niki St. Phalle

or 'The entrance of the only woman in the breast of the group'
(1960 The New Realists)

Saint Sebastian or Portrait of my lover
Shirt with nails banged in
Head dart board, with darts thrown in
Empowering

If you do that
If you knock the nails in
If you shoot the rifle
If you hold the rifle, butt hard against your shoulder
If you shoot the plaster
If the worst meal you ever cooked pours out
Pow pow pow

Saint Sebastian
Is it you too?
It's the menstrual flow
Flou
Femme éclatée

He was a stuffed shirt
'I never shot God only the church'
Christ you pointed the gun at him
and helped Sebastian to die all over again
and properly this time

Tinguely

Now
the henpecked machine stutters
its hooks grasp
spasmodically
He explains the deterioration
of its movement

Little girls in velvet
hesitate press
a foot on the button
look up with dislike at my
dislike
I watch the cycling machine which operates
a mad pram and a nail which scratches
a circle in a metal plate
It is difficult for a child to reach the pedals
The boys seek the greatest speed which
the machine diffuses
I love the boy who holds himself on the pedals
more off than on the seat or
the one who clutches the tattered book for extra
leverage
The little girls are in skirts or their heels slide
off the pedals

Gwen John

On Sunday I relax with Melissa
I sit on the planks of a corner seat in the garden
She is stripping a chair she found in the street
She's sitting on the grass
chair firmly grasped
her back to me
her bare legs spread out
one foot flexed with dark red painted toenails
her skirt with its big red rose pattern spreading
on the grass
her pink sweatshirt, and her long dark hair partly
pulled across by a clip
She scrapes and scrapes away
at the paint
The chair is patchy shades of brown
the brown which approaches and recedes
in numbered tones
"I haven't got the patience for that" says Mary picking
green beans for our supper

Three quarter length young women and girls
by Gwen John
I liked the noses most of all
You don't get the noses and the nostrils in men's
paintings of women
What a relief to see the real self staring at you
but so remote that you can't reach her
gathered in, collected

The Dinner Party

Vulva
"Vagina, vagina! What kind of word is that?" he said
I can say cunt
but I wouldn't to you

Vulva
A creature she said, pulsating, creating
pushing off the plate with every muscle

I was disappointed, yes
Perhaps he was right

This effort can only exist within a limited format –
the plate – she explained

He paused by Emily Dickinson's plate
amazed by all the frills

"And that white sustenance – despair"
    and that white
sustenance
    despair
and that white sustenance
sus
    ten
      ance
And that White Sustenance
Despair –

In the folds of the vulva
"You're very labial"

M stands for the millennium
(It used to stand for your Metaphor and Muse
Symbolic Murder)

In white work
White silk thread on white
   satin
I was spiralling out of Maine
White angles razor

The second time
I took the Judy Chicago tape and
she put the earpiece over my ear
"There's a piece of your hair caught"
And at the end another attendant was laughing 'hysterically'
"It's because we've been working here for eleven hours."

Holland : Ithaca

Holland : Ithaca

One clear morning she knew
that blue sea was hers
was with her beyond the porthole
Although
she walks with the youngest daughter
of the queen, who
suffers, who is retarded
You can see it in the way she walks
on the ship's deck bending
her head

This is our port
This is Den Haag
Not a picture porthole
not a lifebuoy
on a packet of Capstan cigarettes
Here in the breakfast lounge
we eat slowly
Others are falling over suitcases to the
gangway
Someone will meet us
We could stay here all morning

The bay of Dexia and the mountain are one
To you it was just another porthole
'I think you must be Odysseus…'

On deck the princess walks
She will change her name
and marry an American
I seem to remember

Ithaca : The Haven

Suddenly an explosion
an earthquake?
I don't want to register earthquakes
Meanwhile the Lord of the Earthquake, Poseidon
'Seismos' they said in the new concrete house

The sea was calm
A hand held flat
The news came over the ship's loudspeaker
Gaddafi…
Casper Weinberger
"What happened?"
"The Americans bomb Libya. Very bad"
"Yes, very bad"
"The tourists not coming"
I should have returned to my household
'Anything that can happen, can happen to you'

In the streets of Vathi wisteria
fills the Venetian ruins swallows
dive under your feet
three military aircraft flew fast and low above me

    'the good Odysseus awoke from sleep on his native soil. After so long an absence, he failed to recognise it; for the goddess, Pallas Athene, Daughter of Zeus, had thrown a mist over the place… everything in Ithaca, the long hill-paths, the quiet bays, the jutting rocks, and the green trees, seemed unfamiliar…'

HULA HOOP

1986–1989

Inside Britannia

Keeping safe

1

"He threw a brick with such force,
and this is a first floor window,
that it went through the window and
took a chunk out of the opposite wall,
and it's quite a large room."
Later there was an armchair in the street
"Taken up his grandstand view"
George said.

I want to go out and throw that chair away
but I can't
it won't stop there
I can't
it won't stop there

2

"You're not the most comfortable person to be with,"
she told him.
"I suppose listening is one of your skills as a manager.
I enjoy having an audience
but we don't exactly have the give and take
of ordinary conversation."

"I was on a management interpersonal dynamics game",
he said,
"with people from my organisation
in which the centre of power was the centre of a circle.
I took up a position
and so did they and then they drew a circle
around themselves.
They felt that I was outside their circle."

3

We used to think that the more the self is defended
the more it is destroyed

Last night I drew a circle round my body
and then I went to sleep

Relaxation routine

STRESS TEST

What did you notice?
What did A notice about B?
She stopped breathing

In my dream
I was sitting on my manager's side of the table, which never happens, and we were close and affectionate. From time to time we made the gestures of lovers, which surprised the two women opposite us. He put his finger between my lips and I pretended to bite it. I felt warm and safe. But the two women, both teachers, were suffering extreme stress. One was talking about her ulcer and the other's face was contorted by stress. I realised I was looking at one of the self portrait busts by Messerschmidt, the mad Austrian baroque artist, in which all the features are pulled together in the centre of the face. So that was what the expression meant. Because it never had a title.

RELAXATION ROUTINE

this occupies the brain
is entirely natural
no need
to control
it

become aware of your
        BREATHING
say the word 'calm' or
a similar word or a similar
word

you may check the time
do not worry
more
deeply

The Common Good

We are here to defend
decentralised democracy
"And how was the LSD conference?"
"I voted for liberal democrat"

We are so pluralistic
"Consultation means listening
to every point of view"
"And then doing what you wanted to do"

In our eyes
the argument begins and ends

"You wanted to say something?"
"I don't think so.
I don't think I wanted to *say*
anything"

Or, in a dark room,
"Is she all right?"
and his fingers touch his breast which is hers
not knowing where or how far
the cancer has spread

Natural reaction

for Geraldine Monk

'"you have to go mad like us"

Have you got at the truth   did you find out the truth   what the surgeon said   what the consultant said   what the G.P. said what the mid mid wife finds has taken over her life   it goes round and around the cells (soundless) the system   aggressive and you never can tell and the scan doesn't show it's a scam he said we're running a scam   should I pass the wink the nod   it's because they get their stories wrong and they haven't conferred   holding back deciding how much to tell   and when

So you're following her case and you're out of the race   it's autumn castrated   they say you're second rated   it's autumn and jugular here comes the juggernaut   they've falsified the minutes circulating a memo round all of the heads   it says what you write is unusable not bad   it's a yawn and sometimes the director looks at her watch and s/he's here for keeps she's got a high reputation   so just tow the line all of them do including you   and maybe if you try to be positive and watch Marx brothers movies

Grand Metropole

She too will turn
middle-aged

From a tea shop window the picturesque scene not
the imagined hunger
the remembered hunger
the phony war
when he looked across the room for
my disapproval
"McWhirter has been shot. That's one prick
out of the way"
The EQUITY AND LAW sign went up
in flames and he cheered

Later the firemen went on strike

The gold of the sun pulling
you off the white hotel façades
"Was it this hotel,
was it the Grand or the Metropole?"
We look for new brickwork in grimy
reproductions of the avalanched façade
"A great chance was missed"

"They are lowering him down
They are lowering down
Mr. Tebbit on a stretcher"
and I cried
for the courage of the firemen
so long after
their winter of discontent

Equal Opportunities 3

– You get these men coming in with their
   credit cards and their wives
   and she tries something on while he sits down
   and then she comes out and twirls round
   and then she tries something else
   and he tells her to turn round
   and then he pays for it
   Sometimes on a Saturday morning we take twenty
   thousand pounds
says the Laura Ashley girl

– Do you want to work in Laura Ashley?

– No. I studied graphic design at the poly
   and I did my dissertation on pop videos
   I worked in a studio
   I pestered them to let me work
   I rang them up every day
   They let me help out
   I did everything for them
   I was one of those people
   who do what they're told to do
   Throw this away
   Pick this up
   Take that there
   I had a special badge
   but they pestered me
   I was the only woman there

   You know I've got a waterproof watch
   well I put my hand in an ice bucket
   and they all said, "Oh, oh, she's wearing a watch"
   I never got paid
   I just gave up after a while
She finally pushes her hair away from her eyes

– This must be a dead end job

– Oh, yes, but I lost my confidence
   but I'm getting it back now
   I'm getting back my confidence
   I should have been a fine artist
   you know
   or a fashion artist
   but I wanted to try something new
   I'm like that
   I like to try new things
   but it's so competitive
   it's very competitive

Black 1

A man died in Hyson Green prison
in his cell was only a mattress and a slop bucket
an investigation found that he died
due to a chemical imbalance in his body
caused by lack of water
he had tried to drink his own urine

Community charge

– My best friend is a community charge officer.
That's how she said it,
and it's true.

I had a dream that she charged me
three nights poll tax for staying in her house.

And she said,
– Let me ring up Suzanne at the office
and she'll work out how much that is.

She's started wearing semi-precious stones
on all her fingers,
     onyx opal quartz
She used to have such small fingers and toes.

And I said,
– This could be a story
  by Guy de Maupassant,
  about a rich woman who collects expensive
  rings while all the poor peasants are starving.
  And one starving woman begs for food,
  but she turns her away,
  and the woman dies.
  No, the rich woman goes looking for her,
  in a fit of conscience,
  but it's too late – she's already dead.

She turned on our favourite song,
– Me and you and you and me
  No matter what the
  So happy together

  So happy   together

Integrity at Christmas

for Kelvin Corcoran

– I do wonder about his integrity
I wonder about each one
– We must cut our cloth . . .
who could make selling his mother plausible

– Integrity, said the cleric
   To get up on a soapbox and speak out against
   these kangaroo courts, torture, homelessness,
   tinsel, ghetto blasters, jazz

Integrity is a strength at the centre
squatting here in these leaves
raise a family
never see this century

the witch hazel stars
but I can't speak this language
it's too relaxed and precise
not lobelia you mean aubretia

the white pony rolls and comes up red
touch me and I shall be made whole

Hula Hoop

Hula Hoop

Red plastic ridges on my hula hoop
hard ridged band of plastic
               hitting
my waist

red-black brick wall
up the hill to Mrs. Blaggs
with Melvina

we said goodbye at the railway
station where the lines run through
the middle of the town

I counted myself and
kept going
you have to keep the rhythm

a movement of the hips

      whirli

      gigs

watching the Whirlybirds
Buzz and Chuck are helicopter pilots

'whirling, whirling
whirling out'*

Or make it run, scrape
stop and return

it can bend and bend and not break

(After seeing *Girl with a hoola-hoop, Gloucester Street, Newcastle*, 1957, a photograph by Jimmy Forsyth)

* HD

Summer holiday

It was a girl throwing a ball
against the boarding house basement wall

a girl threading my doll's limbs
back together

a girl pirouetting on roller skates
an enormous bruise on her thigh

It was Alma Cogan singing
– sugar in the morning
   sugar in the evening
   sugar at suppertime

It was a girl with one leg shorter
than the other from polio

It was a poster by the lifebelt
– It could be your daughter
lifeless in his arms

She was a teenager and glamorous
a walking, talking, living doll

I'm drinking seven up
I'm paying the cowboy to guess my age
which he does but I still get the silver brooch

Boat Train

always at night the lights
as the train pulls out
leaving my uncle
in the navy

these fragments of light glitter
in the concrete steps
that we climb to the platform
in the speckled glass
of the sweet jar
in the last electric lights we pass

he was my mother's favourite brother
who said one evening
– I'm not feeling very well
and went upstairs to lie down
in his dark blue uniform

Community Art

The sculptor

I was teaching him how to write his
curriculum vitae and he was showing me his
portfolio

Sea shell lamps balanced
on the white parapets
of council estate walkways

The bust of Marcus Garvey

Later, leaning back
you say
– People think I've given up, y'unnerstan'
  They think that because I'm not doing this thing
  right now
  that I've given up and that I'm not going to do it
  but they're wrong
  I'm just thinking of a strategy
  of all the possible ways
  I mean I seem relaxed to you don't I
  I am relaxed but that doesn't mean
  I'm not thinking about what I aim to do

I was already ill so I asked him to take me up
to see the BMX cyclist
It was a lean aggressive boy figure
community art after all
with a large helmet for a head
– You can't get much detail with the fibreglass
He stroked the helmet, sprinkled with glitter

– This should show up nicely in the sun

And I looked at the photos he'd taken
of the boys on the BMX track
They were holding up their bikes vertical
rearing
staring into the camera
from the top of the dust track mound
travelling clouds above them

And then you say
– I'm married I have to tell you
   but Claudine she's very different from me
   my idea of marriage isn't like hers

With your face of Marcus Garvey
at the Black Arts Gallery
broad strokes from the mass
like Rodin's Balzac

Y'unnerstan' what I'm saying?

The giant at Queen Victoria School

Nyome the fire god was a giant
who lived in the sky
– Do you like the giant?
he asked

Squashed
in a corner of the playground
pushing with his fists
at the school wall
head down between his shoulders
one leg stuck down the steps

He made windows in the sky
which were the moon and stars

a little window above his head
has bright green curtains

– Too mannered, said Di
as if it was art we were talking about

Something Chinese in the upward
curve of his eyelids
– Where did you get those eyes?
– Shall I tell you a secret?
　I'm not like other men

I always liked your navel the most
ivory tinged in brown skin
breathe up this slope
breathe in your warmth
a field of flowers in the sun
'not yet affected by agricultural improvements'
switch off the tv

– Do you like my work?
– Yeah
Bob Marley still wrapped
in plastic
– He won't come right
   because my mind isn't right
   I'm not settled
Only the photo
enlarged but glitter sharp
smiles hard
at us

Two spirit people lived inside the giant
and one day he sneezed and they fell
out of his mouth onto the earth
but they got lonely
so they made clay children
and baked them in the fire
when the giant walked past they were afraid
and hid the children
so they came out all different colours

Carnival

or 'art is the easiest thing I can do'

I don' come for the floats
wherever there's a sound system
ragamuffins
know what I mean
it's a Jamaica word
        dance hall

ragamuffins
    are   alone
a way of holding themselves
following the sound system
revolutionary
that's me too

they weren't going to switch off at seven
they weren't going to switch off for the police
they switch off when they're ready
when they've heard enough

Linear construction

'PLEASURE FOR THE SAKE OF PLEASURE WILL DESTROY YOU'
flashed the electronic strip message

– That's true, he said
I must pay attention, she thought

This is the centre of the body
everything moves to this centre
this is the navel
all lines of your body move towards this point

don't touch me
               nothing is separate

'leaving only the reality of the constant rhythm
of the forces in things'*

– It should have been, she said
  a bright brave new world
  like Holland
  but it wasn't

– That's because the destructive
  comes with the constructive

'LISTEN WHEN YOUR BODY TALKS'
– That's true, she said
– Always? he asked
– Always
– Is that safe?

* (Naum Gabo, *Realistic Manifesto*, 1920)

The Shelter Sketchbook 1941

He finds the angle of an arm bent
around a sleeping head

A woman sits up and sees him
Is he real? Is he there?
She doesn't know, she doesn't smile

He is superimposed, a standing giant
in this photograph of people living
sleeping flung on platforms and stairs

Was he right about suffering?
Should he have made them eternal,
these monumental figures of women
timeless, emotionless?

These abstractions are valid
because he hallucinated them
out of the brick walls out of the dust
he rubbed them out of rubble

She lies down and simplifies
into the tubes of the drawing class,
in her dreamcoat and without fear
she comforts him

She says, Give me your fare
and he chalks in the white plaster of her hair

(from Henry Moore's sketchbook
and Lee Miller's photograph)

Miró

for Michael

We are sand and oil

on tar paper

we are forms on a black ground

stencils

black lace gloves

light through dark leaves

on a kitchen table

— Those aren't stencils, he said

scintilla

spangles

for virginia firnberg

and there she was small and small the finger on the drum or is it tambour kept slipping off her skirt i mean it was too big for her lap and the other hand slapping down on it only just in time for the other finger to stop it sliding down she brought down the palm of her hand hard on the stained drum skin, working round the side of it tapping with her small finger and her nail scratching its stained skin and round the edge where the bright steel nails are no not a tambourine she didnt jingle jangle and she is also very confident on the piano and why isnt she going to america and why arent i its been so long i almost could again

i mean i almost remember the day nixon resigned his veins bulging and our veins dont bulge theyre too far from the surface and anyway most of us arent that competitive just territorial like b. who also had small fingers and toes and jabbed with her index finger & i sd her toes were chopped off mine were prehensile like my dads i thought i had his body anyway i mean the hands and feet and face and of course im writing about me now serious like b. and always stroke against the base of the toes the fingers of the feet its the insides of the joints which are the most feeling e.g. the inside of the elbow where the skin is drawn over the wooden

why didnt you tell me to free associate whined the woman who had a curious habit of annoying her psychiatrist by transferring her intelligence onto him so that he was supposed to do all the thinking, it was hard not to get irritated he said and you had to sympathise.

    no lap at all in the lap of the gods the shapeless jumper the red scarf im slipping off again

Deadlier than the Male Cabaret, Cardiff

Anger and white angles
standing at the mike
– Perhaps you frightened him!

– Remember to bend, she said
  to bend your knees
  and relax and smile

for the angels
not Rilke's thank God
but Wim Wenders'
bending so close
so close to the earth

O, Liz Bletsoe
halo of red hair
in your house I slept on
without breakfast

soon you will move to the country
and be peaceful
and live on nothing but housing benefit
though the vegetables did badly this year

I shall bring you six months supply of flour
and the fascination of watching this country die
from the centre

– What do I have to do
   beg?

This morning I walk to
M & S for a BLT and an Israeli orange juice
and then Oriel
au - re - ole
for the new british poetry

from
LINOCUT

1989–1994

Linocut

the tree reaches up
its branches are cruel as spikes
the leaves will have difficult attaching themselves

hands reach up
the arm is severed at the elbow
she has spent a long time drawing her fingers
and now she has reduced them to spikes
the razor is not suited to whorls
and fingerprints

her two arms reach up
and her forehead
she is like a stick
whether bending or reaching

she never painted the walls earth red
but this is their colour
sometimes it leaches to scarlet red
as if she is climbing through a fire

the tree supports a chest of drawers
and above the stove are the wine bottles of the witch
she can turn round and take down the leaves
which hang like cups

the fingers of the tree touch the ceiling
tenderly they push through the red sky
which wraps us up
the sun through our flesh
a hand receiving

Linocut by Jun Shirasu

Solar in Paris

'De la poésie entre les langues'

I am on the road to India
with 4 girls from 4 different religions
Nadia
    and the epileptic woman

I am seized upon or inserted
in thick black lines of the Madonna

        I   am   ellipsis

                  oval

                  el -

                    le

Le Monde, today, 4 mai

        In Los Angeles
        In Sarajevo
        In Germany

she lives one floor above me
                climbs more slowly
to the chambre de bonne
on the seventh and final landing

This is a radio quiz about fashion history
– Were the pockets in the form of a mouth
        or a chest of drawers?
A mouth is the wrong answer

I am learning the tango with Sonia

                    tang
                go

        4 it is

'of Argentine Negro origin with Parisian developments'

        slow   rhythm
         two   times
love me two times
I never leant back far enough
                under his instruction

In Paris tango is orange is still drunk that way   I don't think Sonia Delaunay inspired the advert although my friend Catherine thinks that her first novel the man with the white vw inspired the latest vw ads which are white and say that *someone you love is driving one*   weren't they always lovable he asks?   or even the music on the red audi ad in post communist russia was inspired by her second novel la varsovienne and I sd which car is in the next novel and she sd it's a ford   so get them to subsidise a multi media event

Yellow and black
    Yell   O

on the flagstones outside the centre pompidou
the tiny japanese woman in black rolls
    over slowly with twisted wrists
inside a bright yellow plastic bag
    perforated I think she can breathe
as she turns her mouth is open
                    O

she is caught up with the rubbish
    plastic bags blow past

a hand then her head she slowly emerges
she holds the bag
    stretches it tight between her hands
sucks the stretched out edge
        re   enters
we wait to see her suffocate

I can eliminate the black squares
even when you let the colours fall by chance

The pale face of Hélène, Catherine's daughter, seems to be smiling
and shining at me from the b & w photo on top of the sound
system, where it used to be opaque, uncertain

café dauphinois, framboise, ananas or
mûre sauvage

This morning the sun through the north window

        r O se in Notre Dame

where violet dominates for the long night
She is waiting dressed in violet
I am warm red on blue
I am the south

Leonora at the Serpentine
(Paintings 1940–1990)

saint Anthony recedes backwards
into himself
lowering his eyelids
as women often do

the patriarchs have stopped enumerating
or have they?
is the world of dreams nothing
but newer and busier patriarchs:
digital sequence under our feet?

the tall hats have gone
but the ties are still around their necks
and the hens between their legs
"O henny, henny penny
have a wee drop of whisky, hen"

Leonora is biting open
pomegranates
she is not bitten
she bites with the snake

red is not the optic fibre monotony
of the new mandala
it is her shaped red
cabbage leaves

hiero nym
her sacred name
she is compared to Hieronymous
but not to saint Jerome

O saint Anthony   she's got
your number

Imago

The stones of her body where it lies

        feet

          under

            water

I stood on the shore of Lake Neuchâtel, black water, black night
with my back to the lights of
            the natural history museum

*   *   *   *   *

This is a poem to be superimposed on Oppenheim's 'Femme-pierre': a painting which dates from 1938, when she had left the Surrealist scene in Paris and returned to Basel, entering a period of psychological and artistic crisis that would last eighteen years. It shows a woman made of stones, with her legs in the water. Of this painting, Oppenheim said:

    'A stone woman is prevented from action, but her legs are immersed in the stream … The stone is my inability to do any work, and the only really positive thing is the feet, which represent a connection with the unconscious.'

    When I look at 'Femme-pierre' I see silence and crisis, but also survival and strength.

Masks

When I was living in Neuchâtel, and studying surrealism even, Meret Oppenheim had her studio in Berne, unknown to me. I went back recently and they still don't have any of her work in the Museum of Art.

From a notebook, 1976–77.
'The oligarchy wears a mask. But will this mask resist the assaults of reality? The first cracks are appearing today.' (from 'A Switzerland above All Suspicion', by Jean Ziegler)

The Alps briefly clear, but heavy rain enveloping the Jura.

Dream. The idiot sister. Two sisters. I, the sane elder one, my chin resting on the head of the other. She more beautiful, but with the inwardly turned eyes of the mystic. Downstairs they found strange drawings on the wall – product of a sick or bestial mind. I had let her escape again.

Musée de Berne. Kunstmuseum.
la source de l'œuvre
le contexte de l'œuvre
la postérité de l'œuvre

They wanted to sack Ziegler, throw him out of the university. "You can't be a fireman during the day, and an arsonist at night," they said.

The Alps were sharp and varied again today from the pink of sunrise to the banded colour of sunset. They are like high cloud formations, and yet they are real mountains, I could be there.

"The mountains are hollow with nuclear bunkers, enough for the whole population of Switzerland," he told me proudly.

The Swiss, said Ziegler, are a nation of receivers and concealers.

A girl and her shadow

What I most admire in a woman : silence??'
– J M Barrie

the little girl stands
        up on her swing
arms   stretched   between the ropes

is she going to jump?
      how far will she jump?

underneath in the sand pit lies
      her shadow all frowsty and fubby
spilling out in circular folds

      non-specific like shadows are
blowsy colours permeate lines
         dishwater across a page

pubic hair up on end
    a small green scream of labour

in the background another girl waves
      her shadow above her
         sways with pain

the little girl stands up
    on her swing

Watercolour by Paula Rego

Magia di siepi montanari

the fence has assembled its willing group
of volunteer mountaineers
in this frankly monotonous country
and they break formation   lifting

themselves up into the sky on long legs
held together by a horizontal
each part sufficient
the uprights bending over backwards

aided by fast wind currents
they dance around the corn field
on brittle tracks
a magistery of elements set free

tired of being hurdles
the obstacle course has set off
at its own speed
whose competition was it anyway?

behind this fence I will construct
my house of corn bales
in the living hedge
the field mice will make their home

Coda

this is the way to use gold paint
not for haloes or enclosures
but as cloth for her automatic cross stitch

Etching by Irma Irsara

Two trees for Georgia O'Keeffe

"Shall we look through our legs?"
(woman at the exhibition)

The Lawrence Tree

we are looking down at the sky
        through its brown arteries
        its squid ink foliage
and the stars are closer than the tree

The Apple Tree

whose white flowers are rapid
        separating into petals
        smaller and smaller flakes
of snow towards us on the brown foreground

    we are looking down at the sky

Swan songs

for Rebecca Horn

1

swans open/ and close/ the feathers on their backs
like the keys of a grand piano

their beaks tear grass
grabbing and
grabbing at clover
– Wasteful, he says, they consume very little

they want our favourite space
they are cropping closer and closer
should I stay?
"You were right!
        A single blow from the wing of a mute swan"

2

she strapped feathers to her fingers and stroked her arm
where
     there is the most feeling   the inside of the elbow
the hairs of our arms touching

Mademoiselle, il ne faut pas couper les ailes,
said the woman in the bakery,
when I, Madame, was 21

Il ne faut pas couper les elles
which means you must not cut the hairs

she opens/ and closes/ her wings
a slow grey manipulation of her costume

– But she doesn't fly, he says

only when she flies off the swing/ draped on the pavement

3

he stands naked raising shoulder feathers at the lake's edge

/shuttered/

MAD?

MADAME   BOVARY

MADELEINE   MADELEINE

Ed Ruscha was a sign painter
he had to use words that were of no interest to him
and he carried that experience into his art

I organise information
I break down phrases
I give people their keywords
and teach them how to combine words
Did you find what you wanted?

you can even use a word stem
to retrieve its variations
once I used a three letter stem
which is dangerous and not recommended

It was   MAD?
I searched the whole of literature
Author title text

MAD?

  MADHOUSE

      MADWOMAN

         MADAME   BOVARY

    MADELEINE   MADELEINE

The second collage

1

sleep we knew little of
in the heat of the night
which makes a good charade

you trembling
me calm
so calm I could levitate
as you left me no space in the bed

the soundness of sleep
sounds like

this trembling   "feel my heart"

2

the gift of your letters
late at night
'those sleepless, frail, insistent urges'

3

WHO WHAT WHERE WHEN
WOMEN WHO WHAT WHERE

4

was she called Heather?
she ran to you in another world
talking of her family

saying 'mam' and 'duck'
the things she left
her rocking horse
no, I mean her exercise bike

her eyes the colour of
but that was only his account

5

oxidisation is the process
your body so pale
only the red leaves of your blood
stir in the copper beech
the fine mesh of an open shirt

The dream

it is not good for you to discover that you not strong enough are or not clever enough

you can have it all if you're strong enough and clever enough

"Marlow was my hero. He was absolutely right about a ship's crew. It is an ideal society"

the monkey tricks
          the sailor never leaves home
watching the ropes

"And of course I had seen these places and he was absolutely fascinated"

"I don't think he's even been to the beach"

  and trust to the deep deep element

"Conrad was devoted to his family and envied his son who actually flew a plane in the first world war"

once in a railway carriage he acted as though he wasn't with his wife and children

"My dear fellow, my dear fellow, was all he said to Ford. Now there's literary criticism for you"

"Is she with you?"

in Rye I lay down with the *Reader's Digest*. The view has not changed.

the sea was calm
a hand held flat

Stasis

for barbara

1

she worships olive trees   Athena
sniffing their blossoms from
the edge of Mycenean walls

the lion(esses) at the gate
stand on their hind legs like giant men
good is not their concept

she has a strategic plan
for all the secret staircases and cisterns
hacked out of rock

he makes the sign of drinking
head thrown back
finger curled back

I want you to see this pattern
of cyclopean boulders
this corbelled arch into darkness

follow the girl with the torch
she is unafraid
explores the crevice walls and roof

at the bottom only rubbish
no sacred fountain
I was burning when

I found Agamemnon's beehive tomb
these cool walls
"A peine était-il dans le bain"

swallows have built in the human hive
'O honey bee come build in the empty house of the stare'
and chatter, Ytis, ytis, it is, it is, Ityn

"Orange pressé
　Citron pressé
　Pamplemousse pressé, yes please"

Schliemann's house is a tavern
with a concrete frontage
"La Belle Hélène"

Goering and Himmler stopped here
so did Virginia Woolf
Allen Ginsberg couldn't stop writing to take it
all in

walking away from Mycenae its stones
become the stones of these hills
nothing but camouflage

2

on the walls of Tiryns
to move these boulders
we were alone

levered to make arches and galleries
overlooking the agricultural penal college
where young men jog around an exercise yard

galleries the span of our arms
fingers touch limestone worn
liquid smooth by sheep in their pen

    "Mine is 60 centimetres an arm
     or one metre sixty across"
    'and run my hand as the blind' *

              3

in quiet Tiryns
the café owner is pleased to see us
waiting for a bus and thirsty

she talks politics to talk
"Papandreou, PASOK"
"KLEFTES, thieves" he says

stasis
bus stop

*   *H D – Helen in Egypt*

Saint-Malo

The town

built out of the rock, making use of the rock,
Vauban...
and the machine infernale failed just because
the wind changed direction after they'd
worked on it for two years in the Tower
never seeing the light of day
'Je ne suis pas bon depuis deux ou trois jours'
said the old man
as he left the café

high walls dripping with rain
wet granite as I climbed to the watchtower
they certainly didn't like the English
Surcouf, hero of the Corsaires,
who left one man alive
'because he wanted a witness'

I turned a corner to see the Odyssey
bookshop and spoke to Yvonne
who thought the bad weather might ease the
excess of tourism

The Sea

she showed me 'La femme celte'
who we must imagine across the legends
interpreted by monks
even beyond the Celts – a warrior elite –
to prehistory

as we listen to the force of the incoming tide
I tell you the story of the drowned princess, Dahud
in Ker-Ys, the city below

The King of Cornwall, Gradlon, built for his daughter Dahud
a magnificent city protected from the sea
But the inhabitants of the city led a debauched life
in which Dahud participated
rebelling against Christianity and
something of a nymphomaniac

so that the city, for the sins of its inhabitants
was submerged by the waters issuing from the sea
which surpassed its limits

Since that time fishermen sometimes see the king's daughter
who lives below the waters and swims
amongst the big fish and on calm days they glimpse
the city of Ys, its high walls, its palaces and churches
They hear the sad ringing of the bells

we hear the sad ringing of the bells

Tryst

I taste you
    salt sea
hollow with a taste of nothing

I trace your shell
layer out of layer

your hair clings like seaweed
inseparable

Rimbaud in Cheltenham

I am a contented visitor to a metropolis which is believed to be classical, because great care has been taken with the colonnades and façades and multi-storey car park arcades rising up above my friends with holes in the sleeves of their jumpers. Any words or concepts projected here must compete with the pattern in the carpet, which could be called a percept. Literature is a choice between convention and silence, which provides a neat solution. Amongst the children we see intelligence shining out of their faces as they skate around the ballroom floor, although Madeleine insists on sticking up her long three year old legs and baring her white knickers to the world. The World is nobody in Britain except 1,200 (in the eighteenth century). From the holes in the plasterwork in Madeleine's bedroom I feel new apparitions, the Furies, settling on my skin – Death on the motorway and the separation of Love. And a monologue which only the mother speaks, day after day, unheard to the wall, and includes words about going back to the country. The irregular rapid breath of the child.

anglia

when she closes her eyes at night she can see
    hands on the curtains or else she gets up
to watch tv and she doesn't have to switch it on
    her psychiatrist says it's an addiction
but it made me want to leave for the beach
    and we can't all fit into one pillbox

watching a tractor up to its axles in mud
    you drive into water   your face unworried
    as you dry the engine in the driving rain
surrounded by this farming for sugar beet
    the taste clouding your eyes and nose and mouth
        the price of a watercolour

naked among flintstones where the miner
    is shown bleeding from the haunches
it is foggy and dampy feeling everywhere
    needs dry insulation lining and he hangs out
        the sheet at night which we brought in
            because it can't hang around in here

out on the level playing fields
    it's time for the open floor but she is
        not speaking not speaking for herself
        once about melting ice briefly
two donkeys start to defrost and I split
    an apple between them lifting their lips

we go over the ramp over the dunes
    past swinging babies and yellow diggers
        to the beach where black blocks are striated
        with steel wire   wave defences
when I close my eyes at night I can see the opening
    to the blockhouse and she is signalling to me

Coal

It wasn't the professionals, although I know them, putting on a brave
face, and it wasn't what the miner said, because he only talked about
the nothing, but it was his dialect, which I hardly ever hear now, and
then from my cousin self-conscious, "Ey up duck", that made the loss
in me

a broken red brick black wall
of ghosts and gas masks in the attic
of subsidence and uniformity
of smoke screens and funeral weddings

of Uncle Frank, who used to sort the coal
as it passed along the conveyor belt
who took me on his motorbike,
legs eleven, who called the numbers
who cut ships and vases out of copper piping

who I last saw twenty years ago
stroke paralysed on the settee
singing
 – this will be the day that I die
    this will be the day that I   di-aye

no one wants to work down a mine, like Uncle Albert, who
said nowt as I remember, but read his news of the world
and ate his chips and died the day after he retired

or like my grandad, whose voice I never heard, whose face
I never saw, because he died before I was born

today I looked for a really human sign,
but all they could say was it had to happen

and I'm looking for the dark stranger and friend who comes
with a lump of coal at midnight to bring in the new year
and the new life and my parents lift their glasses in
celebration and tilt back their pointed party hats beneath the
streamers and balloons after the war and all the women are
wearing long new look coats and there is an electric shine
in my mother's coal black hair

18/10/92

Significant moments in the life of my mother

            17

jet hair blown back

glider hanging in a storm cloud

you were the one
        on waterskis
who lost all the islands
        in a tidal wave

patriot games
the reeds bending, the storm gathering
it took most of the morning

            32

a threepenny bit the
doctor held up
   a threepenny bit which
fitted
   the ulcer in your leg
he didn't know how to heal it
no one ever has

it will dry and crust
to erupt again
      the rested leg
the bandaged leg
      the supported leg
the way the blood pushes out of the skin
      from the moment I was born
the life of my mother

Leitrim Observer

      Drum
keeran
     ridge of
the quickening tree

hawthorn white
"like a tin of paint splashed" you said

      no

   not at all

2

Ploughing on Sunday
so that's what it means
we were ploughing on Sunday in our wellies
sipping the white clover leaf
of my first Guinness, Jim Dorsey said
"And where in Ireland are you ploughing
    on a Sunday?"

3

In Memory of Eva Gore-Booth

Yeats was silly

"Would you like to visit the gazebo?"
"I went while you were collecting the brochures"

Eva was wise but caught
        in a form that was not her own

'The tree of life a-glitter in the wind'

        4

    the quickening tree

"Jim Gallagher died very quick
  And just over his operation as well"

Wightlink

'You must muster at your muster stations'
the automatic pilot said to me, the muster-master
whose face I never see

the bar is moaning   whatever that is

the dog is trembling   its teeth clacking
in the crowd

skin is burning
'It is a strong sun,' the forecast warned

we are thrown off by the bubble of air
in an international compass

"We could sleep under an upturned boat
Wrap the newspaper around you"

small boats are sinking   moored and drowning
Sir Georg Solti admires the great conductor
'Major is only a pianist,' he says

"How many of these boats never leave the Solent?"

and you say that I have no sense of adventure,
when with you I have nothing else

tonight I want to see you face to face

Pilgrims' Way

there be wolves here or blackberries bursting
into hatred   I have never seen this whiteness
– Go at your own pace, he said, go –
white horse lifting lip above teeth as we duck

for an overhanging roof   and shake down chalk
here firmer not so loamy not so the mudguards
guard mud on the downs   done roamin in the

– It's a lovely word, why downs? Because they
go down? – asked Nadja   staying below
I say down means up but the pilgrims' way
should have stayed on the top when

there is no staying   always down then
up with no signpost   no road   no path never
thought about the word down before   down
dune   duin   not down anywhere   but over

down is to visit other sacred sites, he says,
or lunch   and why are we ploughing on Sunday
ploughman plods down the loam   my father
my brother to the ox   as we saw high above us

the yellow   DOMINATOR   waits for our offering
but there are wires behind the scenes to lift
                    each grateful limb   my lord

New Forest, August 1990

the principle of moisture
the liquid element
the stream so low
that it barely reached our knees
and having walked in it
it filled with mud
and could not come clean

I slept in the thin shade of a tree
waking in sun again
the danger of waking in sun
"I was worried about you
your face redder and redder"

not such philosophical jargon
he-of-the-trees
who runs in the pine

on the stacked pine trunks
we drank elderflower water
a parting gift from The Sheiling

my flesh glued to the pine sap
"steady, slow and sticky amber drip"

Purple, white & green

– A terrible colour combination, he said

        I'm not sure

I like the clematis drooping on its stem

   as we raise it through the trellis

Did Emily train the reins

   or was she already under turf

      in her purest thoughts?

The Nunnery Walks

> *'What change shall happen next to Nunnery Dell?'*
> *William Wordsworth*

The change is not of canal, viaduct or motorway
        but of neglect, which has swept away
        the paths blasted here by eighteenth century Taste.
It says the path is under repair, but there are no
        signs of repair, only the rocks on Croglin Beck
        where we must imagine the path.
This is all you need to find your way,
        and I watch you disappear, turning
        to look at me, like the red squirrel,
as I wonder where to put my foot
        on the next moist rock, keeping my fingers
        in the sandstone fissures, below the overhanging cliffs.

I do not follow you, and we meet again above the waterfall,
        where you show me the earth slipped steps,
and I squat where it is still safe, offering protection,
        watching the earth's repetition in fractals, its cliff
        contours, its hard red sandstone ribbed with veins,
        like the broken veins of my feet, and listening
        to the waterfall's monotonous glass organ.

Miscarriage

Eden Vale

A few months ago I would have told you that I knew myself, that I would continue the same, make more words. But then there were dreams of birth, and now I am soft, still waiting for the lines to come back…

I was staying in Eden Vale with b. and reading her copy of "Sexual Personae", by Camille Paglia. Everywhere the androgyne is emphasised. "O thou, Atthis, thou of the narrow breasts…" She links pregnancy with illness, as if it were a disease of the body, like obesity. Her own fear, it seemed to me, of her Italian mama and pasta. I am not mother earth, but I was with her then, looking for a place to squat in the deceptive leaves.

And I dreamt of a country woman who told me she was disabled, and had difficulty climbing the steps, and I looked down and saw she was a quadruped, a female centaur, and there was no disabled access to the office.

And I dreamt of meeting three young women from up the junction. "Have a happy, healthy birth,' they said. I was wearing my little Greek tunic, and I didn't know what they meant, but, sure enough, I was having a baby.

"This earth shattering news", b. wrote. It was not the earth shattered, like the paths blasted at nunnery walk. It was the change of nature, of neglect. As we walked those paths, I already knew, looking hard at the veins in the rock, in my body, wanting them to carry the freight

Victoria Ward

my notes said:
she was aware and orientated
when admitted

the drain on gravity
           not working
blood travels back through the tube

this hatstand
        travels with me
dangling a plastic bag

a bruise in my left arm
          where the needle was inserted

"What do you call the inside of the elbow?'

It's the most feeling

curtains pulled around a bed

Stonequarry House

curtains part in the breeze
    a window where glass and pane
        hardly keep company

now we can interrogate the fallen beech tree
cobwebs overwhelm the roots
'Spiders' territory, not ours,' he said

   I see a twisted elephant's trunk
an Arcimboldo painting
the god Ganesh turned over by an ancient storm

the tree's trunk is divided
  where it lies

smooth   grey elephantine   the length of it
I run my blind hand along
   and find it wrinkled   like skin
     or hatched with a pencil
scarred with ancient buds
but there is new growth
   a long branch points up, snout at the furthest end
feeling the sky with its trumpet

"Trees are in people.   People are in trees."
   I asked him if he had ever embraced a tree, and he said that he hadn't

especially beech trees
especially if they're suspended over a sea cliff
    or a river

Coda

Jo offers me a photo of Daniel
sitting proud, rounded and black
on a Japanese lacquer box
"He's my pea in a pod"

Hair washing in the country

(after Sarah Kirsch)

with a red towel out in the sun
warm cloud shadows on stones
acacia leaves

I see through my comb in the light
through my fingers
everything is open

The souffleur

the dandelions had already gone to seed
and two year old Pierre pointed at them
and pulled at their stems

— souffle, Pierre, souffle
I said, sitting in the shade, puffing
out my cheeks and blowing hard

but his little puffs only blew
a few seeds and getting bored
he crushed the seed head in his small fingers

or stamped it under his foot
and then I blew with him
until the seed head was bare

I remembered the other souffleurs
in Suzanne Lafont's photographs
isolated men and women cheeks swollen
with air head tilted up against a dark cross

she said that she was thinking
of Piero della Francesca's trumpet blowers
pointing up to heaven

she said — how can we moderns still contemplate the world
we who are placed at a point from which it is invisible?

we form a world by turning infinity back upon ourselves
we find our place by drawing the world around us
because it is seen from *here* we are led to vision
we point with our fingers
                and magic can begin

Pierre hasn't spoken
he is pointing at the dandelions
we must begin again

This March

for Elaine Randell

'The exceeding brightness of this early sun'
                                    Wallace Stevens

1

match wool to the orange breast
                    to the cherry leaf
her skill at matching colours for his breast

2

the wind this morning
                like a drill
slows the growth
                but only

3

iron age descending
            over Bats Castle
burnt gorse like fine wrought iron

4

the shadow of the sea wall
                its straight line

it was always this light
    this street
with or without his blond pose

Statement

And if I talk about poetic practice
I was introduced to the two line poem in 1968
and I sometimes think I have been trying to play
those two notes ever since like the six
pianos in Piano Circus   which means that
"we're always looking forward"   she told
the interviewer who wanted adaptations of the classics

It might be the secret of joy
which makes people look sideways at you
like last weekend at the Arnolfini
with Bobby Baker licking her toffee apple
gyrating in a red chiffon dress   and miming
"I close my eyes and count to ten…"

or it might be the smell of apples in the orchard
the smell of apples in an old woman's damp cellar
the smell of rain falling in the distance
the smell of the entire village
which doesn't want you
because you always want to build on the orchard

AUTOMATIC CROSS STITCH

A collaboration with artist Irma Irsara

1995–1996

piece work:
a walk around the fashion industry

piece work / the sound of the sewing machine

sounds like *the brook* : allegretto
              (rapid machine lines
              not wanting to let go
              the thread goes on
              table vibration)

brooks
no obstacle is its own
pecking hooks and lifting crooks drills
will not be left alone stop it at will

turn down   seamless   clatter fan ventricles
shutters up and up   human noises   in time   in sequence
peace

on the bottom line
hesitation breaks
low level cardiac
phonemes chink

bangla

back home they have tailors

chiffon rolling around their faces

I'm trying to catch a few words
of Bengali smiling at us
this word for pleating is kusni

mixing up shalwar and kameez
a reigning force for the Westernised
woman who ripples
and third component is the dupatta
which might get caught in a door

tradition   fashion   orange
how long
do we shift and squeeze?

stitching

she is making bridal dresses
which hang stiffly from the ceiling
stepped out with the stitches her dark hands
will into them
from flat cloth to dress which stands alone
she has worked this in

coat hangers float across the room
in immobilised flocks

while he comes along   bends a little
to look
walks backwards and forwards

her back shifts between the light and me

dresses caught in at the waist
for a woman who may turn to her husband
in the Laura Ashley shop and say
'Ceintrée comme tu aimes, André.

she is never still
shaking up the white cloth
a flash of scissors

slowly the ice-cream sits up
and finds its ribbon

above the white desk light
he paces empty-handed

this material of movement in the light
held up by exploring fingers
is a white map
for translucent moving continents

it rises candyfloss
in front of their torsos
sitting up above their hands and heads

they create the new life forms
of white tulle
she seizes it and it rises high above her head
a great frothing between her hands

sometimes she waves her hand sideways
to release her fingers
before pinning some corner of stuff
back under the machine

light on her hands
on the back of her hands
as they bend
fingers pointing down
pressing down
meeting at needle point
below the machine head
the donkey pump

overlocking

we make bridal dresses

with silks and satins from India

difficult material

it gets dirty and damages

this is not a normal dress

hand finished

handpressed

the final and special overlocking

he doesn't know anything

I want you to do some overlocking

overlocking needs to be done

you said two or three minutes

you've had that

it is enough

we have work to do

overload   overlook

the factory owner

I'm Makis. I'm Greek, from Corfu. Most of the factory owners here are Greek Cypriots, and there's rivalry between us. We make blouses here. We know what women like.

I deal with German manufacturers. We know each other for a long time, so once they've got the orders they spread it about. Give you 2–3,000 a week and that's it.

It's the worst business you could get into. We make blouses £2.70–£3. Buy a lot of trimmings. Working for peanuts. Manufacturers and retail make all the money. A lot of the work done more cheaply now in the East, in Romania. The manufacturers send it there. But if you do good quality work you have a chance to survive.

A *lot* of skills needed:
cutter
overlocker
a machiner
buttonholes
buttons
pressing
checker
button up and clean
driver

See this line here, on the pattern?
The cutter makes one mistake here
and you ruin the whole thing
finished.

With loud music they can't talk. Because some people they like to talk.

The manufacturers doesn't like Fonthill Road. What happens in Fonthill Road? You can buy there for £10 what C&A selling for £25, so obviously they can't allow. No way. Fonthill Road Fashion Centre very, very small people. I don't deal with them. Only the big stores in the West End.

the machinists

'We worked from 8.30 a.m. in the morning till 12.00 o'clock midnight yesterday. We were told that the ongoing job had to be finished, because the boss was losing money due to the delay in the delivery of the finished product. Next morning, workers started to work at 5.00 a.m. I could only make it at 8.30 a.m. because I couldn't wake up earlier. That evening, I finished work at 8.30 p.m. because I was exhausted, but the others carried on working. I don't understand how the others could bear this situation. I have to listen to the gibberish talk and the demoralizing music all day. Even if I finish work at midnight, I can't go to sleep straight away when I come home. I have to calm down and chat with friends to relax myself and refresh my energy.' (Finisher)

'I love to come to this park, watch people, children, trees and drink a cup of tea at this cafe shop. But can you imagine that it has been six weeks since the last time I came to this park, because I worked seven days a week from 9 a.m. to 9 p.m. for the last six weeks. I feel so exhausted.' (Special machinist)

(from *Primary health care needs of the Turkish speaking community: survey report*, 1995 by Ferhat Cinar. Healthy Islington 2000.)

Fonthill Road fashion shops

looking

Come and have a look
Keep an eye on your bags and purses girls
Come and have a look girls
Keep an eye on your purses and bags ladies
All right girls
Don't be shy now   come and have a look girls

2

Half price sale ladies on first floor
Have a look upstairs
We have all sizes
Beautiful dresses
We have all kind of evening party wear
Sale upstairs ladies half price

the importance of sizing

Two young men are running a fashion stall in an alleyway on Fonthill Road. A young woman comes along with an older woman, probably her mother, and is looking for the right size of dress on the open racks.

And one of the young men says—What size?

And she says—26 size 24.

And he doesn't know that size and he turns to the other man and says—Do you know what size 26 or 24 is?

And the 2nd man moves his hands along the rack until they go off the end, and says—That's it. 10, 12, 14, 16, 18, 20, 22, **24, 26. BIG BIG** That's the big one. No way no.

And the 1st man turns to her and says—You're 14 in't you?

And she says—She's not.

He shakes his head and says softly to me—Twenny six.

Dream designs

Fashion Fever
Message
Impressions
Cyprus Hill
Orchids
Vision of London
Branded
Metro
Panache

Lace
Flirts
The Cut

Dream Designs
Branded
Cinderalla
Flickers
Opium
Shadows

Flamingo
Lagoon

Pyramid
Shapes
The Cut

Cockney Touch
Touch of Class
Flickers
Just Right

Spider
Accolade

O Cinderalla
Dame
Drendie Girl
Evona
Gemma Trimmings
Gypsy Girl
La Femme
Loriana
My Lovely Lady
Prima Donna

Vogue

I trust my instincts
Who do I dress for? I wear only what pleases me
(Oasis for Vogue, fashion shop window, Regent Street)

trust trust	trust my trust I
instincts	natural impulse independent of
instinctively	independent of reason
instig	
sting	or experience
credit credit me	these things are t/rust

instincts trust me

who
who
who do I
who for
WHO?

dress	dress	dress for
who who	I?	
wear	wear only	what

only wear what

pleases   pleases   please

                                    me

what pleases
                            please yourself
pleaseth

pleasure — | F

        pain —

                principle —

                        beyond —

                                death — | F

the mind resists unpleasure

resist   this

        I

Warehouse

what you pick up from the mud are
sequins and beaded motifs
where they are thrown from
trimmings and edgings of the canal
views of concrete render   losing their grip

a stitch marks length and must be regular
like a small flag among towers at Canary Wharf

the best view in London is not the underpass
of sighs and security although
in my dream it was this glass stairway
to the light railway at the wrong station

between the columns only
the brightness of her sari
and a child lifted on her shoulder

'endless calls deep into the night warned me
that I had upset many important people
this was something else more sinister
a kind of urban cyclone'

manufacture makes stitches too small to be visible
forgotten backdrops like roman roads
                                       and runways

the coronation flag in the shed shredded with age
these white threads are bothering me
these white threads scratched across

                                         the red

write the dress

white gloves

her thin fingers are
illuminated with a new kind of x-ray
a mysterious white light
revealing their structure

the woman who left these gloves behind
has disappeared
the dame is dead
and next time she will have a name

and then her glove
will send men out into the streets
after making them aware
of the limitations of their logic

and they will follow these hand
prints in the paper
beyond (as we agreed)
the mere economic necessity of work

to find the sense of their lives
where her white fingertips touch down
and white blood flows round
invisible to closed eyes

buttons

1

too large pressed up
  airholes
    blow through
      whistle
        my practical olive:
          buttons are
            hard pressed
              dark green she wore:
                round the back of the teeth
              it must have a rim
            meeting lips
          everything for a grip
        space between
      the upper and
      the lower circle
    smooth pressed
  feeling your
inner warmth

2

small
cuff ends
undone

twisting   chipping
stubborn

—it had to be her
her buttons are always
half

        white pills
        snap at them
        all the way down
        the dress

        —at that epoch
            I was more romantic

3

play   tiddly   tiddly

            wink

press their edges

            jump into the cup

the girl's dress

is a palimpsest
an overlay of loss
of memory
time and
landscape
where is the dress?

1

the idea of the girl's dress is
an elevation
a bouquet of sweet peas
on the steps of the orangery
above the cast shadows of the lawn
in the white sticks
of the treasure hunt

2

translate the dress
read the dress
write the dress

3

que c'est jolie
la robe de la petite fille!
la petite robe jaune
la petite
little one   little one

4

I am reading the yellow dress
in the wide field
of a cold Easter wind
and it is as bright
as I want to be
as bright as the sun
melting the coldest Easter eggs
on this beaten
beaten track to white Sunday

5

language in its layers
irregular patterns
it grows and language
is crystallised
radiant stasis
of its international yellow
cannot cover a winter field

mini

a modicum of decency
in the days of the mini
(V&A gallery)

when first discovered we knew nothing but
while our fathers played with toy railways

my worst nightmare was to arrive at school
in a pink dress not the uniform blue

I always wanted my own skin
not realising that this is also fashion

the phenomenon of fashion involves the idea of a covering
a covering which overlays another covering
that of the skin

and then that june night on the terrace
when I moved his hand back up to the frilly blouse

of my breast and away from the end of my
pinafore mini   slight layering of tights

sat in his lap I was not preparing for life
but another quotation

and he said   you should do as I have done
and go into a field and scream

crushed velvet x 2

1 *black crushed velvet*

it was black crushed velvet
shining unisex

        the irregularities of
it is crushed for
        fingers to press down
small ridges
rough to the
        running along

trousers made for sliding
        between
or sliding up a hand
        in the metro

I was so thin
they called me the stick

he was a violinist
        I saw a copy of Honey
        Honey   I said
        Honey   he said
and I was slipping out of

        slinky

                slunk

2 *yellow crushed velvet*

for Beverly Semmes

bright yellow crushed velvet
      square neck
does nothing for you
      tank top
      headless
above

        restless nights on pink rayon sheet waves
            marooned by fat yellow cushions
     which are my wheaties and

        baklava

          honey

fetish

I glued my own soft curls to the doll's bald head
and the hair changed nor did it help the doll
which became a hybrid
everything living was in the fingers
and the faces written on the fingers
at least one of them had to go to market

when Terence Davies fills the screen
with a creased white sheet
it is as good as five minutes of linoleum
through a rain soaked skylight
instead of Gone With the Wind
I would have a loop tape of my mother
singing you are my sunshine my only sunshine

pheasant startled out of maize
the inlets too dangerous for navigation
not because the water is too shallow
but the land is always moving
and the maps are too slow
a finger of water takes me to the mooring
wind through gold rushes

in the early morning I am alone
in Mother Julian's chapel followed only
by the video surveillance camera
and an automatic beam of light
someone must have arrived before me
and lit the first candle

is the shawl a burthen or a delight?
she showed me how to drape the excess cloth over
my arms so that it doesn't trail on the
mais non it maintained her status for an entire month

as nothing else might have done
un vrai cachemire murmured madame
as nothing did

the nothing that he drapes upon his arm
and wishes for the thing itself

every poem is a story

                                    masquerading

as an object

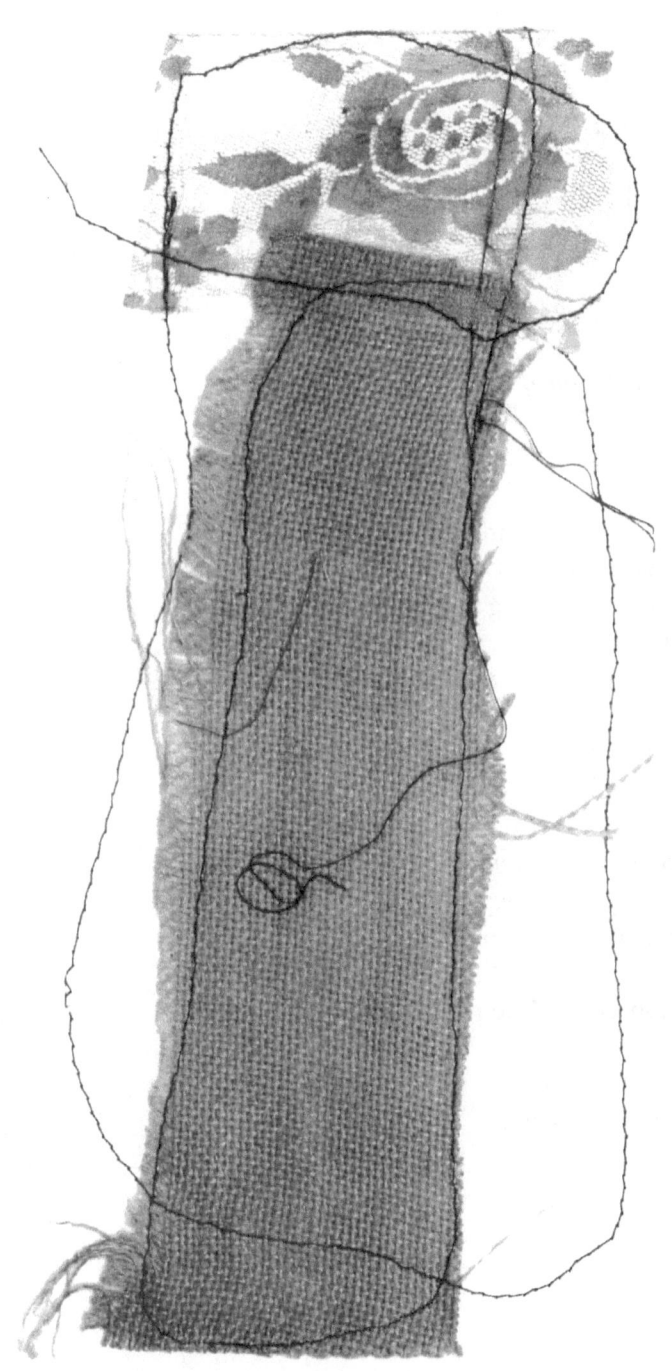

Veronicas

Imprint Veronica
Veronique
my black eyed girl
protégée

a fashion for ghostly imprints

      of intelligence, he said

pass me the handkerchief

we have lost our trademark argument
and strap marks too
however thin the G string in a hot sun
mediaeval cathedral   graffiti
    his hand in that word

the speedwell genus   violet (heart's ease)
with often blue flowers
a cure for scrofula   from scrofa the sow
or the action of a torero when
without moving feet or legs
he swings his open cape to divert

the apparition of this face

sweeping
her gesture to dry   dry out
a dryer-upper
of vapour

sail
veil

thin transparent material
and then she took the veil
and wrapped it round
this fashion for residues
posterior petals united
posterior sepal wanting
sped daguerreotypes of
mercury vapour development

she was projecting again
he was the photographer in her
he was the sweating in her
a great sweat broke out in her
it had to be mopped up
with a man-size tissue of
pansies and lace

she frightens herself
with the dying part of herself
in the procession
which she absorbs in the linen

Mary Wollstonecraft in outer costume

first you will see the purple and the gold
it is not pleasant to have the devil
delay the search for meaning
I am distrustful of myself
coming for the conclusion of the sheet
before it is written into
the outer garment
the all enveloping burqa

had I allowed myself more time
then you look up
I could have written a better book
then you realise that it is all of a piece
for not having done justice to the subject
with the gold helmet and grille

'That's really tiny isn't it?'
this is a particularly decorative version
with lank hair, black stockings and a beaver hat
for everyday wear
looking through a fine mesh gold grille
before it is written

notes

p. 189 'white gloves' includes a reworking of the incident in André Breton's *Nadja* when an unnamed woman leaves her glove in the Surrealist Central.

p. 196 'yellow crushed velvet' was a response to the American artist Beverley Semmes' installation 'Kimberly'.

p. 200 The starting point of 'Veronicas' was a series of daguerreotypes by Patrick Bailly-Maître-Grand.

p. 202 A letter by Mary Wollstonecraft, in which she complains of her difficulties in writing *A Vindication of the rights of woman*, is interwoven with a description of the burqa, on display at the V&A.

Automatic Cross Stitch was originally performed, with a slide-show by Irma Irsara, at the Feminist Aesthetics Conference in 1995 and then at other venues in London.

PRIVATE WRITINGS

Vermont Journal, September 1996

with drawings by Peterjon Skelt

Adele's   private   writings
reveal   a   woman
trying to make sense of why she is unhappy
when she has everything:
    …there is such selfishness
connected with everything we do. Why is it
that that feeling of self always seems to
haunt me?

barely a foot
a foot barely
        in both camps

cycling towards another century

spruce up

swinging up between maple trees   so high
then   down   come   I

the heaviest wood is lignum vitae

the heaviest word

it takes girl power to work the horse ferry

    – do you want to be a circus rider when you grow up?

    –when I grow up I want to be the horse

hissing and grimacing

cycling towards another century

she is wearing her jellies and walks in the water

or jumps over the beam of
    the Philadelphia   touching it with one foot

water slowly leaking in
a float for cannon   she hugs the cannon

arms around its black mane

hang my arms around its neck

crossing lake Champlain
don't shoot until you see the white of their houses
don't use estuary english

fear
                            and
fear

jellies and walks

'purple clover, Queen Anne's lace
 hair hanging down around your face'
who is the girl with the horse's mane?
golden rod, black eyed Susan
stands on the deck and looks for her man

'just as far as my poor eyes can see'
blue, blue chicory

a beautiful young woman, Jane McCrea, was scalped by
one of Burgoyne's Indians. The exact details of her
death   remain

              hazy

but the effect of her murder was to shift sympathy away from
the British and to the rebels

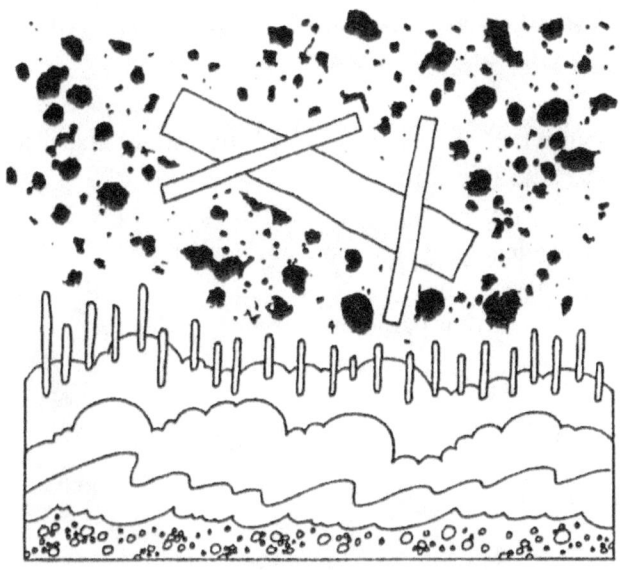

stands on the deck and looks

Mount Mansfield, once compared to a moose's head, and now to a man's, named after a long dispersed township

disputes about whether we have reached the chin or else it must certainly have a double chin

Susanna at seven leaps over crevasses somewhere
indoors somewhere on her head
– show me, where is that panic button?

should we sink it for future archaeologists?

you can't float the nails, Susanna
only the wood

                                      the word

lignum vitae does not float

the only way I can get back in is to fill it with water,
swim into it and then bail out

Miss Piggy lifting skirt
    on the lumberjack's barge

this is folk art not
the mermaid prow at Shelburne Museum

lily leaves pushed up in the last log roll
hulled and ribbed
already on the bottom

sand in the marine archaeologist toy
sorry, I'm breaking the mood
- I want that one and that one and that one

switch off the tv

folk art not

leaves are copper plated
good conductors but will come to rust

grass   knots   cross

cradled by the lily pond
that's all I can remember of Rousseau
slap   slap
the slap slap of bare feet on lino

small waves on lake champagne

– she steers like a doll today

I am rocked by the hou-hou of the old freezer
life in the freezer
or mallarme and macrame

the white noise of children
– and then he tore his head off
   and pulled out his brains

the lighthouse keeper's wife went into labour that night and by a prearranged signal the doctor was alerted on shore. however, the ice was too thick to launch a boat, but still too thin to safely bare a man's weight. the doctor and his assistant decided to set off, but as they walked across the ice it began to crack and they were swept away on an ice floe. the lighthouse keeper's wife gave birth unaided. later, when her husband died, she applied for and was given permission to tend the lighthouse, with the assistance of her children. she did not keep a journal, but this is what she might have done everyday

NEITHER THE ONE NOR THE OTHER

1998–99

A collaboration with Elizabeth James

Normally, women only exchange remarks to do with children, food, or perhaps their appearance and sexual exploits. These are not exchangeable objects. Yet to speak well of oneself and others, it helps to be able to communicate about the realities of the world, to be able to exchange something.
—Luce Irigaray

The goose is standing on my balcony accusing me of neglect

Here is a park, an ark and golden eggs

Reversionary factors marked the nest

Personally I don't get the benefit of that fecal decal
twitching regularly in damn braces & killer pain
still plump for morning after pillow flight & a gander at the papers

Re-ver-ver-verting to typist

Reverberations of the fine feather nest enhancers
always have to end with a free floating eiderdown

dare we settle / snow in april / derry dancers

Verdigris trials plump her keys

VERDIGRIS TRIALS PLUMP HER KEYS
claims Elsie's old man, for love or money

She was severe and variable in her strokes

Just keep on apologising for my slides

and the recognition of her breast stroke
one foot/ a plastic bowl

a butterfly net
turning after 25
metres again, love

it's not a race, Beginners II, it's not
a family even

to recapitulate at Glassonby
the song thrush
it ... rolls
turning my hand
'a rondo' he said
what are these other episodes
these other subjects?

yes, wawy
martens, swallows and swifts

lakeside in urbe
refrain to egg
thrift, wallow & the shy parting
curves of crest and speckled bib

œuvres r us

ups and ups
always the second syllable

bim-bo bim-bo bim-bo
and he said it's
sal-vo sal-vo sal-vo

applause & heavy rain save their appearances
I volley, though my nerve is broken –
there is no true spondee in English poetry

Pa   pa   pa   mime all plaudits
and reign savours volition
bite into the sprinkling of powder

a/men   a/men   a/men
underlined impatiently (he said)

(these are your words)

Ditch the index, ditch everything else, and write something

a.m.

mirror and single
contact lens
tip o' my index
a reflex flinch
I put it in

mark lines
her eye eyes
poor authority
straight heir
clings to me

ma-
man
maudite

this is my ditch
the love is warty

mo
mor
morwyn
      (or

          if you prefer

          the breton morgan)

     sea
rising
     drift
ditch the index

love more than
se
a monster

oh frances

morgan is my
mother

I do not   prefer

– scales aweigh!

it was those wide melodic leaps
she was scurrying rapidly
up and down the scales

eye-slash-lash scrape her swelled lid
nights after a taxing form filled dishabilly
     datasurge

ventures testing riotous finances
poetry day is worse than thought for the day

no upper-body strength
no upper-arm strength
no body-on-the-floor strength
no over-the-body strength
no under-the-body strength

she says that he says it's a dance about falling

really needing that time for herself but had to blame it on
no permit without kermit
and he says Yes but still my point
still   my   point

Ulli Freer was at VI
reading a sequence called dense
which includes the line
'there is no ego in collaboration'
it seemed egoistic to ask him about it

I also liked the line
'can't see the wood yet feel for the tree'
can't see the word
my elliptical Os
you have to see the word
      I mean the wood

and so we could
fall for the trews
and creep to free

or prefer
singing together
of mount abora a a a

o labor
it spurts, falutin
ab ovo
    a mon avis

we need to approach the pastoral with care & remember that it's not a convenient utpoa

                       we need
              we need to approach
        we need to approach the past
    to approach the past we need we need
                to approach the pastoral
we need to approach the pastoral with a car
     o approach the pastoral with care
           we need to poach the pastor
              to cart toward aporia
approach the waste & pare the weed to the
                               core
                to catch a parsnip

and remember that it's not
and remember that it's not a
                    convent
and remember that it's a con

ut poesia pastoralis

her oaks are tiny things in plastic tubes
like premature infants
sun catches their leaf shadow

the trees join heaven and earth
and the world below
on Blakean linear terms

I feel for their sinewed trunks
a muscular infold
cannot identify this tree

in the forms she remembers
from Nellie Nature

stock cubes / mach ants / chest hair

vend art / hew low / Lakes

fort sinus / Amis Larkin / tide history

for her : read only : Neat she

All the mythic versions of woman…
are consolatory nonsenses (Angela Carter: Sadeian Woman)

spiced parsnip   passive hole   lead detail
pound each   cut yew   broads
flat business   Hughes Morgan   post millennial
:   his entire (net) tribe of collectibles lodged here

(In terms of the travelogue, this is the (my) road to Norfolk.)

next morning I brought up the Sadeian Woman
and it quite put me off my sex

ni l'un ni l'autre   I do & I don't

his black weight on her calipered body
she said it was a girl's view but there must have been something
wrong in the phenomenon

The Sadeian Woman was Carter's vindication of the rights
she could have written a better book
given more time

everything was showing
as if showing was everything

the chemise en scène
her apparent
parent
rent

a bone structure
in repair

"original floor covering of tapestry embroidered by two of the princesses
4 ladies made a replica of it, which is identical but the colours are fresher
Osborne House, a real family home but some of the rooms were too
opulent for my taste" (post card from my mother)

    everything was folded
    as if
    skirting the word in lime green
    her wainscot
    wave partition
    parted painted wagon
    wains   coat

    wains
        cot

Cottage my foot.

Queen Victoria had him brought to Osborne House, perhaps because filming would not be permitted at Balmoral.

Short breaks are available.

A converted outbuilding the other side of the car port from the landlord's bungalow.

If the weather was bad I would read *The Marginalization of Poetry*.

'Mrs Brown' was taken by him to visit the poor in their own homes, laughing happily.

Gratton Dale was full of bullfinches and goldfinches, and it had snowed on top of the mud.

He also acted like an unpleasant bully.

The females can be seen to have shorter sentences.

still the narrative unfolds one's sympathies shifting under his hairy blanket

Hearing the bells at midnight we went to stand among the locals outside the Duke of York.

In exchange for Labour the cottar shall get access to the coterie.

What might you have.

The palace to boot.

I was sinking between Victoria's tyranny and Brown's paranoia. I had forgotten her reassuring banality.

It's nice to have options at a bus stop.

A controversial 135 feet high tent was raised over two acres of the town's holiday centre.

When I had flu I read *The Marginalization of Poetry*.

'Mrs Brown' was taken by him to her predictable, if politically sound, crockery.

We were somewhere on the Quantocks in the red river.

She also acted like an unpleasant bully. Peel was forced to resign.

The male has a longer memory.

I couldn't help thinking that Cinderella was a touch more traditional than Angela Carter's version.

Hearing bagpipes at midnight we joined the studio celebrities.

It was not the widow's choice who she should remarry.

What might we have.

Finding it extremely hard to open up this poem again

Finding it extremely hard to open up

```
        b      i              m      u

   o        t           d              t


       r      e              i      c
```

      or bitten by blanket stitch
      which is an orbiting style

      running up against
      all that joined up thinking
      in the social exclusion unit

      there is another clause
      there is another cursive

      *

      tumulus umbrage dilates
      cabled bearing borage

A little difference / making a great deal / different / interest rates / fall by half / of one per cent / over / all over again

Can you credit / The Millennium / "our anniversary" / your birthday, her / last ever PEP / We herd / Fortunes in floristry / flow / owing

Seam non compliance will attract penalties
Food in your freezer
. Insure.

the word stress is less stable than you think
the women were all dressed in black tie
as Olive made a dash towards the subvocal
I like her line of suspension points
....

I struggle with my breath

Try the melismatic:

I str - u - u - u - u - gle

or ED:

I Struggle with my Breath

My mother could not catch her breath
I struggle to speak on their anniversary

dum dum dum dum b-dum dum dum dum

sing then, at
least sign

t tss   t tss   t tss   t tss

                                      listen
oh mother we love you ~~get up~~

This collaboration was conducted by e-mail, during the financial year 1998–9. The epigraph is taken from Irigaray's essay 'The Culture of Difference' (1987) in *je, tu, nous: Toward a Culture of Difference*, translated by Alison Martin (Routledge, 1993). Among the poets' interests and occasions were: the music of Hildegard of Bingen ("those wide melodic leaps") – her *Ordo Virtutum* was performed at the Royal Albert Hall on the 8th of September; Merce Cunningham ("a dance about falling") – his company performed at the Barbican on the 8th of October; William Blake (his "linear terms"), especially 'The sea of time and space' (the Arlington Court picture), 1821; Louise Bourgeois ("his black weight on her calipered body…", "everything was showing…") – her exhibition at the Serpentine Gallery in December; *Mrs Brown*, a film about Queen Victoria's relationship with a Scottish gillie. Angela Carter's *The Sadeian Woman* was published by Virago in 1979; the 1998–9 pantomime at the Lyric Theatre, Hammersmith was based on her version of the Cinderella story. *The Marginalization of Poetry: Language Writing and Literary History* is by Bob Perelman (published by Princeton University Press, 1996). Other poets quoted or alluded to include Olive ("made a dash towards the subvocal") Custance (English, 1890s), Frank O'Hara, and our esteemed contemporary Ulli Freer. "VI", a.k.a. Vertical Images, Vegetal Irradiance, etc., is an experimental poetry and music venue in London (*Neither the One nor the Other* was launched with a reading at VI, 15th April 1999).

FP/EJ

SOMERSET LETTERS

1993–2001

with drawings by Ian Robinson

For my mother: Connie Boogerd, 1921–1997

1

Dear Elaine :
From this window you can usually see the sea, and sometimes the Welsh coast on the other side of the estuary. Today it's concealed in grey white mist, which also lies across the Minehead holiday camp, with all its funfairs. The colours are in the foreground. A woman walks down the path to do her shopping. A well-built woman, wearing a white shirt and grey skirt, she balances her handbag on one shoulder, and her shopping bag hangs from the other hand. The next woman looks younger. She wears a green jacket and I think she is more concerned about the weather. A single bag hangs from one hand, a tapestry cover. They are gone too quickly for me to observe for long, although they have a measured, unhurried pace. The lane begins with a pole and three official plaques attached to it, all washed white by time. The top sign is round and shows a bicycle. It's supposed to prevent bicycles. Now a man walks up. He does not carry a bag. Difficult to judge how old he is. Fifties? He has a warm, green cardigan, one hand in his pocket, and he looks around him in an observing way. Neither of the women did that. He is tall and strong, a deeply tanned face, although it is hard to see his features through the distortions of my window pane. The next down traveller is also male, but older, white haired, and with a faster stride than either of the two women. Like the first man he has one hand in a pocket. And then a woman, grey haired. She has the largest black bag, hanging from one hand. Is this the shopping rush hour? It's 8.50 a.m. Either it's always the women who do the shopping, or else the men find ways to conceal the fact that they are shopping.

I'm thinking about the tradition of male chastity of thought, to which I owe some allegiance. It isn't, of course, literal chastity. Someone young, too late to see if it's a boy or a girl, I think it's a girl, flies down the path on a bike, red jacket, small rucksack on her back. I seem to spend a lot of my time encouraging girls on swings and bikes. But not, I hope, for the purpose of achieving male chastity of thought.

"Don't throw the water out", my mother pronounces, very distinctly, but it's already too late, because he has. In the garden opposite a woman is pegging out the washing. As she walks back to find the pole to lift up the clothes line, she lifts both hands, as if in prayer. She then walks back into the house, with one hand raised to her head.

It wasn't his fault entirely. I was the one caught between competing traditions. I still couldn't quite believe that emotional completion could only take place, for him, in art and not in life. She goes down again, shopping bag on the left hand. Soon there will be nothing left to do except distinguish between the left-handers and the right-handers. The blackbird scolds and scolds from his vantage point. My father claps his hands. At first I only hear the clapping of the hands. Why clap your hands at a blackbird? But he does, as he opens the gate, as if they were disputing the garden. My father is going shopping. He takes the car, and drives away. Or is it the female, the brown bird who is scolding? Suddenly she flies to the gutter above my head.

The iris

I forgot to pick the iris
says my mother
it's black wet December night
time to shake out
the tablecloth

she does pick the iris
by torchlight
That's the trouble
if you don't pick them
they get devoured by slugs

petals on a tray
wet and floppy purple veined
a yellow column
at the centre

Hollow ways

the hollow way
always led to a village

not the Holloway
of ambulances to the Whittington
police sirens
that never get through

*there must have been
so much activity*

to an oblong house
with its back to the hill
for protection

everyone has windchimes

to a house with its back to
the sweat shop

sweating up Cat's Scramble
this is a bridle way!

the deer lead us on
emitting radio signals

2

Sign it, not Sig it. The letter was lost between the van doors. Lifeboatmen do it with two loud bangs. My loins are aching. I like this phrase. I read it in *Passions of the Mind*, an epic biography of Freud. He walked all night because his loins were aching. The acorns are too large falling out of their cups. I shield my head from the bombardment. He was whistling through the cup, where it was trapped invisibly at the base join of the two middle fingers. His brother-in-law looked at him the show-off, piercing our ears. He couldn't see how it was done.

– I didn't know they could be so troublesome at that age. – Where did you live before you lived in Minehead? – Doggy's enjoying it.
Joan tells me about a programme on the radio called Last Wish, and a friend of hers who had always wanted to ride on a hovercraft. So they arranged it for her. And she was also able to live at home on the sea front, until three days before she died when she went into a coma, and then she was taken to St Margaret's Hospice. It's very good the work they do, although I don't think that charities should run homes. They were meant to just provide the extras. Is it true that 50% of a charity's income goes on administration? Are you hypnotising her? Would you like to have your tummy stroked? Oh yes please, he says, from between his braces. I think that charities should be abolished.

Fierce red taking charge of the branch, and the tree is inhabited by birds like an advent calendar. My mother bending down to tie her shoelace and panting. I just can't see the logic of it, she says to my father. Statistics are statis – statis – statistics.

We've got what London takes! I'm from London. I want to know what this is.

All the girls were carrying crosses as they hurried down from Hurlstone Point, overtaking me effortlessly. There was talk of blood and suffering. I carried yours down to the beach. What are the crosses for? She showed me the spirit level at the centre of the join. Oh, you explain it.

They told me that I had to have my eye out, and have a plastic one, Joan continues. It won't make any difference to you, the nurse said, you're blind anyway. Of course it will make a difference, I said. I can feel this eye moving.

England were pretty pathetic last night to be honest. Flies are droning at high speed, intent on the Grand Prix. It's very difficult to write nature poetry now. To keep it simple without being metaphysical. Two lines from Harriet's poem, 'Brancepeth Beck':
> under beck bank duck
> flies sudden up

The pure northern vowels that my father taught me. Are they harsh consonants and dark vowels of the Seafarer? I think that the vowels must be light. They are eyes in the clouds, where the light comes down and tracks a low green field.

Dry fur

this white rain
these fine black branches
    we pollarded
the father

*

always pick out the background colours
I looked everywhere for the silvery beige
but had to make do with the cowpat colour

*

we are all fluent in BSE
sponge brain it goes
cross field
field crosses
Jacob, Jacob
slaughter the cars

*

into your tangled pink

*

fur of dry
moss under my hand
your stomach stiffening
against mine

Park range

work, he said, we can work with them
we have to reach those people

with a display of life in the iron age
and this may seem over the top

thatched huts, caravans and chalets
we must trust the crown estate

buzzard blows between sitka spruce
it is legal to shoot from the queen's highway

a noose around Lorna Doone's neck
to hoist the statue onto its plinth

each one trying to claim this is their history
not knowing if it is any of our history

we cannot swallow the new estate
returning to retire in embarkation

deer hooves down to the pond

lifted frog head motionless
mummery at the crossroads

3

He is standing near the pond as if trying to work out the exact degree of thaw that might or might not have taken place. She says that he needs spiritual help.

When I open the curtains a man lies dead in the street on his back, as though he might have slipped on the ice. He is covered with a sheet, and I can only see his hat, his shoes and a black labrador tied to a fence post. The labrador seems to have difficulty standing as though it too had lost use of its legs. My father thinks the dead man might be Mr I who has a bad heart and a black labrador, but there are so many people with black labradors.

I am trying to decide whether or not I want a gender. Even now this subject can still alarm me. The women I am reading would like to be genderless, though still by way of writing about cunts, or the most impure labour, abortion and miscarriage.

Nobody wants to work with computers. I dreamt that the head of IT had been sacked, and the man he had sacked was reinstated. Walking past the whortleberry bushes I think of him. He asked me enviously what whortleberries are. Are they the same as bilberries? One summer, I said, for geography we ate wurts and drank from streams.

He tells me how amazing it is that the ice has thawed in some tubs faster than in others. I say that it must be to do with the colder parts of the garden. "Yes, but it's not at all where you would expect it to happen!"

4

I need a grammar that will link the channel tunnel to the need for an extra groin in the sea wall. I mean groin, depression between belly and thigh. The minimum number and size of groynes necessary to economically contain the beach material is reassessed by the design architects who realise they will have to see things in the light of October's storm, for which they were not prepared. The park warden is urging the sea to break through the shingle ridge and create new openings and lagoons, which look lovely from above. You cannot economically contain the beach.

Swallow the sun before it sets. Short moment. Yellow grass and mounds of sawdust. The old life.

I am reading Brenda Chamberlain's account of her life on Bardsey Island (Ynys Enlli), and the strong dark lines of her drawings. She says that the nature fancier is the town dweller with a sentimental view of things. Her sentiments are wild and believed to be archaic, but, like the boat to the island, they cannot always hold water. Nature leaks through excess diction. The seal's nose is nobly aquiline. She listens for a tongue still vocal in the dust of the island, when we know from a long way off that the dust is still vocal in the tongue.

A brief history of Somerset

'do withdraw themselves unless they have livery and wages to double and treble what they were wont to take, to the great damage of great men' (*Statute of Labourers*, 1351)

great damage

great men

the tenants performed 182 manual works called Churrys
a churry or churr was a turn or a piece of work worth a farthing
cerran/cierran   OE to turn
all turning is work
the road was called churway, which later became Cher
it became a chore
or a char in Bath, circa 1971:
Theym all the same they night nurses, they do fill they jugs too full

Minehead

                                                      Mine
                                  is   mine
                                          mine is the

  myne   mynadd   meaning top of the hill
                       from the Celt
she went back before the Celts
                        to a time
                                    no but
barely had she reached
                       these mines
had travelled with her
                              mined
further
                   mind in search of
the quest for psyche
                       tried once in the british library
east myne
        west myne
is just a circle on the hillside
                       where farming interferes

with the Saxon theory
                 which begins with my head
                    myne   heafden
                                myne head
if it's my head how can it belong to the hill?
                    this is broken by the two halves
not mine
                  but mine head
that makes no sense
                  except as the head of a mine

there is only the hill
      which is built on but not into
except when they quarry for sandstone
      red cleavered surface mining

these are pretend mines
      the ones we pretend not to see
not in this language

     head hide
     heed hired

Seeing oaks

1
Her love of her mother. Her mother's gift of language. We were looking at dead or almost dead trees today, trying to decide where we could plant trees for my mother and what kind. Mr Carslake offered two yews, but I don't really fancy yews. They were always in church yards. There's a very practical reason for that ... to keep the cows away for their own protection. And it was a very useful wood. Not that they are really poisonous. I remember Hanley, was that his name in Ruskington? Hanwell. Yes, he ate a few berries just to show that they weren't. Because there were yews at the bottom of the school garden …… Or walnut trees, he said we could have walnuts. I've got nothing against walnuts, I suppose they're native. But I was thinking more of oaks, or maybe ash. Don't you think, oaks? He examined the branches of a great tree in a clearing that looked almost dead, snapping off some twigs. They could clear this away.

2
pine needles
wish bones
these two must be separated
not in the same house
skin flurries
wind or the furies
sleep creases

he said that the two oaks will grow
and if they die
they will be replaced

and I imagine my mother
watching them
my eyes her eyes
these gaps of sunlight
between the shifting oak leaves
and that is true of any oak tree

Coleridge notebook

the sun at the end of the garden
drops quickly but at right angles
to the bookroom blue
evening sky behind the cedar

these eighteenth century letters
to my brother are maxims
though we would have seen martins
following all my letters

Kubla Khan or carry the can
brom shurs @ carrot
black polythene on goose by patch
it wasn't subsistence farming

a tallystick to evade his creditors
sun through the shingle ridge
on the grey salt licked grass
or the sword to buy me out

nameless dread
              dread
do they cull bones here
a poet's life leads nowhere

at midnight on north hill
the stars were closer than the firs
held close against the cliff edge
there where your foot fits

the black rocks if you cover them
over if you cover me over
if I cover you when you go
to Britain and the caves are
              uncovered again

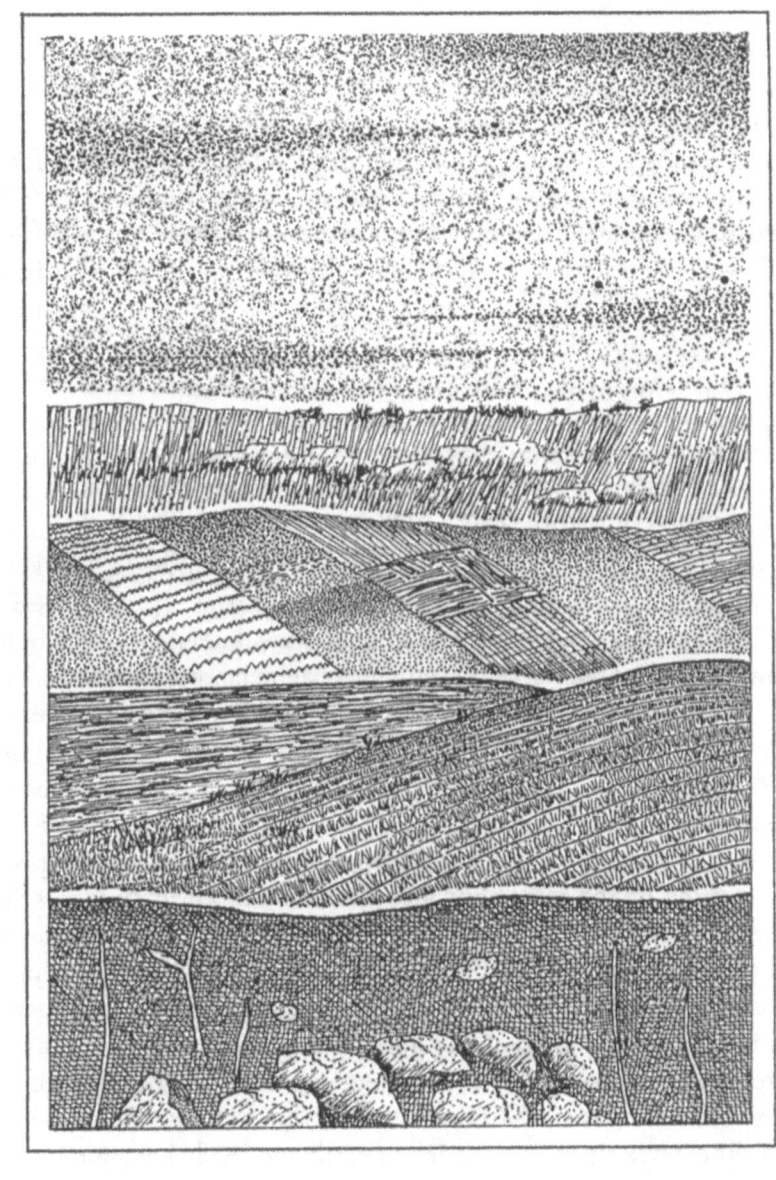

5

Unpruned prunus. The banging of doors, his. Let's not have too many of these frills. Soon I will fold up my mother's clothes and take them to the Red Cross shop, where, in February, she sent me with clothes that were not good enough for the bring and buy. More than nine inches of rain fell during the 24 hours following the evening of 15 August 1952, one of the heaviest rainfalls ever recorded in the British Isles. Mrs Ellen Jenkins grasped Dilys' hand and nightdress so hard in order to retain her hold on her daughter that her hand remained clenched for three days afterwards: Harriet Bridle. That series of abstract paintings is just exactly the clouds above the estuary until a seagull gets in the way on the sea wall, which must be a relief for the readers, as they have got it entirely. Someone asks which are the clouds and which is the sea, and obviously the sea is up there and the clouds are down there. They are so neatly folded that there is nothing to fold up, nothing at all, only things to take out of her handbags. She kept everything. Holland after the war. All the old pens. I am not really moving these objects around like a chess game, because then I would know their identities. They have increased the land drainage level to allow for the flooding, and the Sedgemoor beef farmer lost 40 acres in the summer. He thinks that without hunting we lose touch with ourselves, with nature, and our place in the food chain. The new type of jig saw puzzle is a three dimensional mansion. He's been up there all day in his room with it and he's got as far as the first floor. The speed of discussion on the net is always a problem, but more than that is the anxiety that not enough has been said. Perhaps it is better to go away and think about it, and remember this crossroads and a place to pick whortleberries. A gorse bush had fallen across the narrow cliff path, and it was difficult to climb round it. On the second day it was still there and I pushed hard on its prickly thick stem until the root shifted in the soft wet earth, and it stayed against the bank and did not whip back. There was a pervading smell of earth and the lightning revealed 40 foot walls of silt. My father wants me to write in the memorial book and I resist and think only of clichés, who loved these woods. But I imagined my mother seeing these oaks, and say that I will write something 'poetic and original' and he is glad that someone will. He praises her calligraphy and she says that the entry can be as long as we like. Those are the scars that were her eyes, on the tall slim trunks of the silver birches, up into a blue sky. Always prune the rose bush so that the eyes are facing outwards. The paintings are called 'Broken horizons: shattered dreams', but I think that she liked the yellow in it.

6

I dreamed that the Fine Feathers dress shop had moved from Bampton Street to an underground car park. A front room shop where smart good as new dresses for older women, like my mother, are occasionally exchanged. He follows rivers, as much as possible, making up his own path: a surveyor who has lived in Bridgwater all his life, five yards from the house he was born in. He has always counted himself lucky, and he knows the trig point exactly in metres rather than feet. It may already be privatised. There is no need to turn over the map. It has to be better to live in one place and he seems calmer now, telling me that the female frog is huge and hangs full length, belly engorged and red. Gorse in flower and the stems are still across the path, and my movement of them was not metaphysical. I certainly didn't think hard about it. She has news of bullying at the middle school, and how the two girls can't go there anymore, and who is back in hospital with his back to be reconstructed. Reports show that service users do not want local home helps as too much will be known about them. This is another reason to leave the pronouns vague. You don't have to draw every branch, just give an impression. I wonder which impression he means. This path which is a stream and leads up hill. Style of live water, but it doesn't have to be flowing all the time. It must be very old if the bedrock is exposed. Is this the bedrock or just a human construction? The red water flowing round my boots. You can't always follow the river.

7

Butlins, I mean Rank, own the foreshore. She knows that because she once complained of wheelchair access to the beach and was told to write to them, and the following year they had installed a wooden ramp. 'Inevitably, in due course, we will wake up one morning to the news that the whole of Minehead has become Rank plc behind our backs' (*West Somerset Watchdogs*). The crunch of sandstone sand, strange moans from my old trainers. Buzzard low in the scrub trees twists along the marshy ground. I don't like to do seasonal work, the young man said, and he is advised to do the New Deal. The Reverend Mr Davies must have kept all those utility sheets because they hadn't even been taken out of their wrappings. They're terrible to wash and iron. You have to pull and twist to get them straight and catch them just right with the iron. With Minehead we move to a more measured tempo. Turner shows a sweeping view over Blue Anchor Bay to Dunster Castle with North Hill and the Blue Anchor Inn in the foreground. Sweeping my view around a blue lagoon, somewhere in Italy. Dad asks if we have any brown wrapping paper, forgetting her excess of wrapping paper. A golden beach and cliffs not yet affected by caravans, where blue shadows cross delicate dry land trees. What kind of tree is it in the foreground? He says he thinks it's an artistic tree, an oasis tree. Rugged mountains strain upwards after some violent upheaval, with the castle on its high pinnacle. O Minehead. Now I would call you mother.

8

If I pull the hood down with my hand, the water runs down my arm. I am the river. He said that Hughes became prosy and more himself in his last work, but it was not the life of the river. I thought I would die that day. Twenty-eight of us set out and only eight came back. You should never go anywhere on your own or without telling someone that you've gone. At the carol service in Dunster I could hear her singing, standing beside me, her deeper voice, the last arrival in the pew, shorter than me, even with her hat on. She was not distracted by the sopranos. I had to let the sound go, let her go. He wanted to send out the lifeboat for us. The horse rider's three lurchers chased around the mongrel, worrying from head to tail. Each hunt report ends with the phrase 'the hind was accounted for'. My daughter's with her dad following the hunt. She didn't want to go, but said she would. He may be riding though he's not a confident rider. I hope he falls and breaks his neck. The skyline of Minehead changed this week as a controversial 135 feet high tent was raised over two acres of the town's Butlin's holiday centre. The Skyline Pavilion, as it has been named by the firm, forms the centrepiece of a £43 million redevelopment of the 165 acre holiday park. At night it is a white and cartoon ghost. Suddenly it was nine o'clock and the bell ringers. The wind sounds like the onrush of cars, losing her soft words. All the plates and glasses. No one to wash up. Harriet relies on the words – the way they sound, the way we hear them or don't hear them. The gaps and the breaks.

Blurred passage

Castellated barbarians
          shoe mud

white out
under steam
wet rump
sheep sign
under powered
water whipped
hair stranded
foot-turned
                    hassock

some found a right of way
swimming beneath the new pond
a release of water

North Furze Hill, Hoar Oak, Long Chains Combe, Pinkery Pond
Saturday, 3 April 1999.   OS 714453

the very title
the Right to Roam
is very misleading
it is not a general right
and the general public might be
understandably misled
                    Tom King, MP

each individual case
to be negotiated
there is one access agreement
sudden loss
sudden loss of influence

      urgent mist

clearing to

        smell of almond gorse

              whortleberry shoots

            small

                white

                  wood anemone

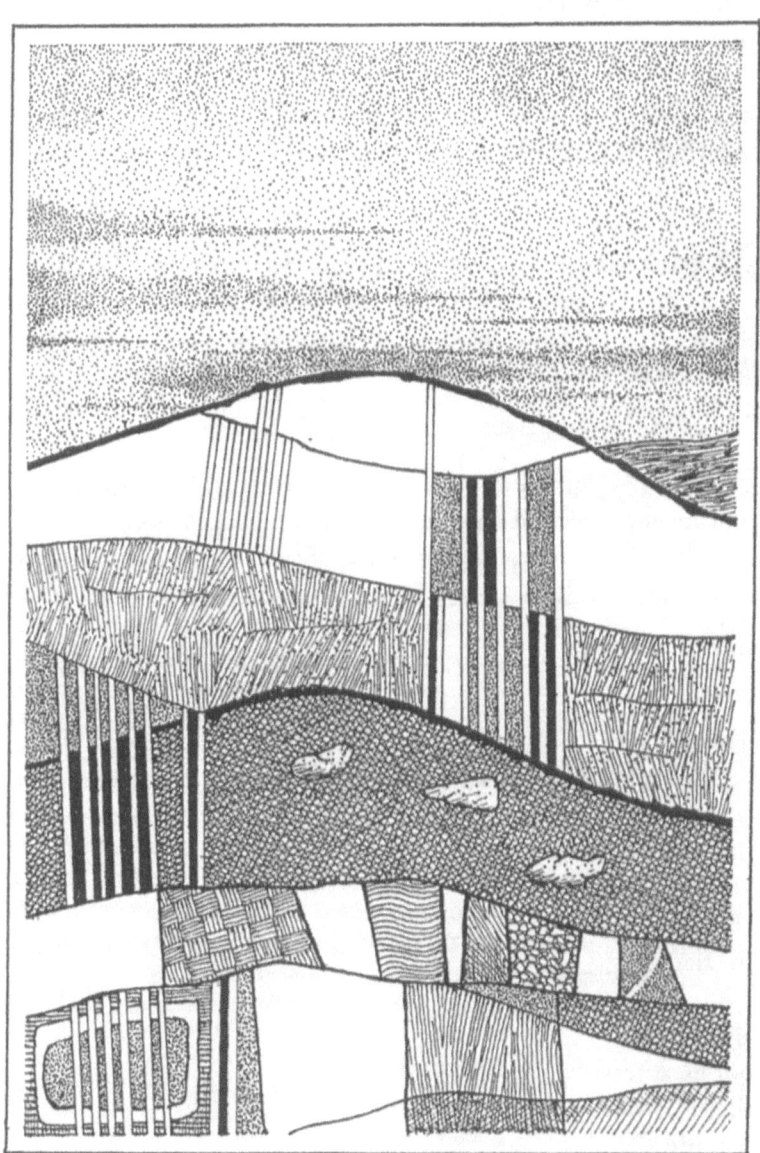

Blithedale postcard

'I want Chris there, otherwise we can blame the cancellation of the meeting on the foot and mouth outbreak': mouth parted over mobile phone.

I had hoped to leave the rusty iron-framework of society behind me and find again in Somerset an available foothold between fiction and reality. We had stept down from the podium; we had closed down the spreadsheet; we had waited impatiently until it was safe to switch off the computer.

Dear Colin, My comment on the lack of otters and red squirrels was not meant as a criticism, or indeed as an expectation. It was an absurd reduction, or a reduction of the absurdly expectant human being, until we find what is.

No footpaths, no bridleways, no pleasure grounds. We spent our time trying not to look like walkers and rolling down our socks. The jeweller said he thought it sounded like bureaucracy, as I looked round his shop and kept hearing baroque.

Foot and mouth disease (Amendment) (Regulations) 2001

Insert clause ( )
Delete clause ( )

No access
No public access
No rights of way
No common land

Substitute ( )

Remove from the face of the Act

                                                     remove from the face of

at line number twelve, following

The background is
>				overgrown
The purpose is
>				unknown
and is worded in such a way as to leave total discretion

There is a useful provisionality in the categories of social being and a minimum £5,000 fine if apprehended.

MINEHEADS

no two mineheads are the same

since 1959 they have been obsessively photographing imperilled
                                                          industrial structures

these delicate giants stand over the shaft entrance of mines

photographed under overcast skies

it is part of a lift installation, the purpose of which is to
deliver raw materials excavated underground

no two mineheads are the same

(from *MINEHEADS* by Bernd & Hilda Becher, MIT, 1997)

9

The bright sun through the new stained glass window throws its coloured light on the floor. Twisted strands of red, like a blood rope, are cast upon a diffuse sea blue. In my dream, which I scribble like my dress, I had to take a blood sample from my friend's arm. The syringe was huge and I had to aim for that tiny place in the vein on the inside of her elbow and I was doing all this while we were swimming underwater, our hair swept back, some blood escaping in the water. I look up at the new window, and the sinful woman at the well with her back towards us, dressed entirely in red against a blue background. The tall Christ figure facing us is clothed in white, and therefore absent on the floor. They live on the flood in Lynmouth, she said. It's a pity because they could do so much more. They won't allow anything to be changed. The windowsills were wood varnish, and we wanted to paint them yellow, but they wouldn't let us. We'd moved down there to open a restaurant, but then, in the October, my husband dropped dead. So which particles will I be – the clouds above the sea, or the new pearly lighting effect of the seafront enhancements, already tried successfully in Biarritz? They are enhancing the sea. Falling behind the rest of the group we talk for a long time about the merits of cremation or burial. His main argument is that it would be better to be cremated alive, than to be buried alive. I used to have a romantic view of cremation, the scattering of ashes to the sea wind, and I had not realised that there would be so many ashes, like the weight and mass of the body in my arms, or that it would take so long. They must burn the coffin as well, he says, unless they reuse them. It was only C's unexpected recital of Swinburne which made it possible to finish. Yes it was more music than meaning, but it was also more lullaby then lament, more mothering than moaning, modulating her feminine and masculine rhymes, a moderation around us.

stitch trivetting
tope scree
bank scrimming

sten endeavour
given dipper
flare plea

10

Admiring his gooseberry trimmer, he was telling me about all the flooded places where he got stuck with his car, trying to get back from Taunton, before finally abandoning it near Blue Anchor. Once near the flood waters lapping into Gliddons' car showrooms at Williton. The root of transgress has to do with walking across, trans gredi, although the argument that follows is not about transgression, but the natural pathway of desire. I hadn't realised that playing Scrabble has more to do with preventing the other person from using words than with making words of your own. Following our short scramble up the hillside into thick fog, we began the descent. "Look", he said, and I saw this gleaming thing, which I indignantly thought was the bonnet of a van parked illegally on the hillside. When we got closer I realised it was the surface of the Aclands' granite memorial stone, with its faded Latin biblical inscription. The landscape architects in Hackney used the term 'desire pathways'. These were the paths that people actually took, rather than the ones that had been laid out for them by civic architects: imagine some small square patch of grass, surrounded by high rises, with a muddy track diagonally across it. Our architects aimed to incorporate those tracks rather than ignore them. For a moment, when I read the first page, I thought you were writing in a different country, someone else's, hers in the city. The tall joy pink flowers of the vibernum, and the purple bladder campion above Lynch. Is this just an exercise in naming flowers or else does it reduce to her common pink metaphor? These units of language keep us constantly guessing, like the first steps of desire.

below the sunline
                      whiteout
                                                into white rook aus

                              ancient birch

that's a good girl
                              good girl

air
                            ere
                                                          err

Somerset letters : note

This series of poems and prose began as a correspondence with the poet Elaine Randell, who lives in Kent, and has found new ways of writing about the social realities of life in the country. Another poet who influenced its writing and who shares my passion for the 'outside' is Harriet Tarlo.

I'd like to thank Derrick Woolf and Tilla Brading for showing me other aspects of Coleridge Cottage in Nether Stowey. I'd also like to thank Ian Robinson for giving me a copy of Brenda Chamberlain's book *Tide Race* (Seren, 1996).

The paintings *Broken horizons : shattered dreams* (page 261) are by Diane Andrews Hall, and appear on the front cover of Lyn Hejinian's *My Life* (Sun & Moon Press, 1987). Memories of the Lynmouth Flood of 1952 is by Harriet Bridle (*Exmoor Review* No. 39, 1998, pp 16-23).

The words on Turner (p 263) are taken from *An Endless View: the artist and Exmoor* by John Yeates (Exmoor Books, 1995).

The poem 'Blurred passage' (p 265) is a response to Gavin Selerie's poem 'A line engraved', from *Days of 49* (West House Books, 1999). It celebrates the 1949 National Parks Act.

'Blithedale postcard' (p. 268) refers to Nathaniel Hawthorne's novel *The Blithedale Romance* (1852), an ironic account of a utopian farming commune. The letter is to Colin Simms, poet and naturalist (see also *Paravane*).

PARAVANE

Barbara, the patron saint of architects, was looking out from the tower in which her father had imprisoned her for refusing to marry the man of his choice, who was not a Christian, when she noticed that the tower was structurally unsound and might colla[pase at any moment, so she decided to stop worrying about her marriage and her religion and focus on how the design might have been improved, but as she could only see a very small part at the top of the tower she had to extrapolate
                              downwards

Paravane day
for Mary Herivel

gather into the chariot bearing
sing low sweet
parabola in time high emptied windows

way to go
way to go home

or does this show
our 'general direction of travel'?
(new set of overheads)

here he is at the gate
with his ultimate ticket
leeve mooder, mooder leet me in

never leaving a message
on her answer phone tape

pause b_____

overgown gathers dust
testing gradual perfect sight

notation spot lights flash across and over
coming to light under your fingers

a slight undulation
at the western most edge
one in ten
seeing light in rain waves

coral cantor in a minor key
love, mum

Ground O

Prone veering
Bell sign
Enters Fuji
Bell sing

Grasp maws
Programmed claws
Dance over pyr ric

Features focused
Eye tongues
Prest glass
Dance over lights

Less than thin
Steps away
Test bed
Of
Filed
Filings

Be a part of it
I want to

Blow your horn
Fit the battle of

Sally sally sally's army
Find us now and at the hour

Skies over
Heavens over
Fuji

Arterial tree
Gird her soft toys

Calm/
Ing piano
Issime

Ethelberga, patron saint of scaffolders, conducted herself heroically in a plague, and founded the first religious house for women in England. After her death at All Hallows, she appeared to one of the sisters and they designed a reliquary space for her taller than average skeleton.

Underwriters

24/4

Underwriters
of intimate scale
it is under written

as she found her way to the Bar
two bombs caused
great
                      damage

displaced dealers
on a temporary trading floor

she was looking for St Ethelberga's
in the ward of Aldgate
where no one lives
especially the common councilmen

a common workman said:
turn right
and you'll find it

what's left of it

between high walls a narrow space
of boards, clay and sca   (f)
                                        folding
yellow on her red shoes
washed away across the pavement
       falling over bollards and pipes

Bowyers

commissioned
by the Worshipful Company of Longbows
to a window
in memoriam

in memo
insert crest
insert Crécy, Poitiers and Agincourt
famous
                                        vic
                        tories

she felt the ideas could
be taken further
in contemporary glass
the bow treated in an abstract

manner yew leaves and the long curve
grows and moves
bows lend themselves
to rescue
yew leaves and the long curve

                                the
                                    long
                                        curve

                                            yew

                                        leaves

                                    yew

cutline

9/2

prose of the Jubilee

lines from her forehead
press down to the bridge of her nose

INTRODUCE SOMEONE TO OUR WORLD

It's harder to enter Number One
through its transparent stiles

"the absence of colour emphasises structure
and geometry"
Contemporary Applied
Arts

I dreamt that our rich host was kindly showing me round his art gallery, and then I saw you slumped in a corner, blood on your face. You were fortunate – he was paying for your rehabilitation

praying for your rehabilitation

"WE CALL IT SHOUTING"
he explained
this use of underlining
or capitals

the danger of walking or cycling
past scaffolds in squalls
or standing with security
under a red citigroup umbrella

blown back
follow anyone
under the glass

Capital Wharf
no memorials
no libraries
no books

this free paper:

the bean counters
long summer
banks pet
banks put
      STOP
to exile of Thatcher
island of lost soles

FORGET THE REST
CLICK ON TO THE BEST

leaving soles on the sally ledges
peer above the spikes

      AN UNDERTAKING
Which, under the favour of GOD, shall contribute
STABILITY, INCREASE and ORNAMENT
smudged line of cement
           bisects the stone slabs

    con   tribute
    stab   ility
    or   name
    which   under

Number One
is a Periodic No.

at its centre

```
          im     press
          be     spoke
         sen     sation
        hirst    emin
        enter    tain
        intern   ation
         mas     erati
          be     like
         bed     room
          en     joy
          se     cure
            tow (e) ring
```

Stonenest street

a twig is hanging from my gutter
should I hang out of the sash window
could it be a stork's nest on the chimney?

these bulbs with spider legs
or catherine wheels
will not lie down in the rubbish earth

hardly time to dry the sheets
between one visitor and the next
between one visitor's words and the next

buttercups are replacing the lawn
I distrust ranunculus but love butter
reflected (repeated) under her chin

what would we do if half the people in this street
died of a mysterious illness?
let me call the co-operative and engage our baby skills
who would take notes onto their lap?

11/9

it's three bells
amplified
at the Arts & Media School

someone is breaking up
axing out
paving stones
in the quarry
malet bangs

the crocodile moves in
and spills the nuclear family
easing out the corners

I speak to people
They stop me on the street
They say, Betty, Betty,
This isn't right
He must come and speak to us
In the event of any war

there's a red curve on my cornea
a strange sickle
from the street's dust
which allows me to see everything
with my customary myopia

the archbishop designate
is worried that we see everything long range
and only God sees close to
he must be thinking of sparrows
which no longer fall
due to double glazing

2

few people at work
emails for absence
notes from a small office
messages from the Transition Advisory Board
we are in the process of being abolished
for the last two years

It's been endless all morning
Angeline complains
Nothing but personal accounts
or George Bush
or stuff on Iraq

no transition without abolition
messages from the
Modernisation Action Board
modernise
moder
mode
mod
mo   mo

mooder   mooder

Fluid Canvas

> "movement is slippery"
> MERCE CUNNINGHAM

a constellation   dances
                that

a constellation of his hands

the puppeteer

are they sacrifices on his planet?

 holding patterns
 what is your holding pattern?

fiend (?) to the spine

not quite landing

not quite arriving

tendrils

aerials

wires

                expand on the roof
to infinity
to sofuosity

she probably did Greek

                                epi

ascend bodies from clatter

ankle hold
          spa shold
                      spec
               spis

          space
spass

                spent

s   osteo
gather some   more   fArSiTeRnOdIsD

     asteroid
     friends

                              avoid the hot spots

Subject: Re: Semtex
Posted by FP

note on semtex

from the village of Semtin
semtex is stable and shapeable
eludes sniffers and sensors
a god send

(this information is not secure)

semi   text

seme

seam

semantics

se
man
teme

                                                              tic

                                                                 tics

                                                                 ticks

              semitone
same text

                                                                  tex

seminar on semtex

semenal

semsem

sesame

simsim (Arabic)

semitar

sempstress

sem   stress

semper and simper

sempre forte

Semele

        a

se   mantra

Post scriptorum

St Ethelburga

Church ravaged by IRA bomb reopens as centre for peace
Ring for appointment or climb over lighting wires and hand tools to disturb the final workmen

St Helen's

should I write about   abolition?
these angers
in a 'godless' church
don't bring my focus
bring your focus

no/ in these white walls
no faces but scrolls
within me such
naked
brutalised

not poet but pret
ready to be depart
ed a men

                                          all the stained
                                      glass shattered
                         inventor of the spirit level
                                        the word cell
                        and the universal joint
                                      Robert Hooke
                                        lost in the blast

                    the roof lifted, ^ the organ badly damaged

St Mary Axe
~~(the Baltic Exchange)~~

A plate glass 'gherkin' designed by Lord Foster for Swiss Reinsurance

When first I saw it from Crouch Hill, I thought how did it appear without my noticing? And how like a great beetle rearing up, falling back, although the antennae were its cranes ^ a beetle out of its alignment like some demented dying lad ^ bird

Close to are
diamond panels
within larger diamonds
large shining steel diamonds
with smaller black inner diamonds
and behind those you can just see the
ordinary rectangular window office panes

winter wonder land
walking
avoid obscure chemicals
in pret a
ready to take

US says Iraq is in breach of resolution
FT 20/12

Sad-	The
weapons	dence
threat-	better
orally	securing
scientists	tary
Blix	include
Bush	Other
repre-	nothing
US	but
pushed	hindered

Coda

for G

last night we were a perfect u-
joined after two weeks absence
laid in by a skilled marqueteer
two thin panels of wood
dovetailed
double
diving birds

Garrigill

1 Nov

Dear
that day of the Helm wind you will remember
past Rotherhope Fell carrying you
and the belated birds of prey

                        belated   *belated*   *belated*
                                                      birds of prey

                            a cluster finds the forest

                                           that fell
                               those birds of prey

                     and you with no phone at all

Stonenest street

1 Jan 02

Dear
I was dreaming of (escape)
dreaming of that high rising bank
your birds of prey
vague in its outlines
a different quality of darkness
a line of fells
can't see above
the underlines in your letter

can't see above
the line of address
and you are illegible

? Red Start

can't see the words
the woods

<u>*pair*</u>
<u>*why*</u>
<u>*here*</u>

stonechats

Garrigill

23rd May

broken bones in
r.h. & wrist
in a fall on Fiends' Fell

                                                Eden Vale
                                                25th May

                                            urgent letters
                               clarity of the left hand

                                            phone numbers
                                                  given

                    this line of clouds
                       across the fells

fleece snagged –   on wire
contours –   that children draw
to emphasise –   a separation

Black burn

binocular
coincides
the bird
and the shadow of the bird

these adjustments
I can make
though still struggling to
distinguish
the male and the female
which is quite different
again
love

harrier (female)
in quad lights
banks

buzzard (female brown)
outmoving the lens

hands and feet
balancing the contours

words underlined
downstream
stressed by spars

Tertia at St Mary Magdalene

The stations of the cross, the tour and retour of the church. The pre-Raphaelite Christ who needs a helping hand. This is a very good likeness, Veronica. Like and like and lekker. Who likes the likeness has a kind. And this is the third time she has walked round and got up.

She turns the chairs one by one, deftly, in a single motion, until we are all facing the back, because we had begun by facing the front. We always begin by facing the front, and we are ready to fall further in that direction, on our knees. We want to face the front because we feel that there is a direction to follow, and it is with some reluctance, then relief, that we turn to the back. We all need something to cushion us, both sitting bones and cartilages. There is not much comfort in these cushions, and perhaps that is why they were called kneelers. She hesitates, kneeler in hand, as if looking for the resting place, but they were not made to fit.

When we are turned we can see that the great rear window has no stained glass, and therefore is all light, so that she is almost all light. Her intonation, intended tones. Which chapter and verse is it? Should she be reading from this book? How were these pages moved together. Will these words be the words of comfort they always expect to hear, before they turn over the chairs and faithfully balance them on the desks. The upturned seats left them standing and safe from the perils of this.

This too is a sacred language, because it is made so, and cannot be heard in those other secular venues. We never saw letters unless they were illuminated, and the letter that she and you give fronting us is quiet and a rounded face in profile, although there is a tumbling I figure in the margin. The missing pronoun is thee, and we believed in thee, because we never heard it, like the e that is silent and all these other excess letters. Let us not introduce too many new words, because we are trying to turn around the same words. So I will come back to thee, and a dialect so disused that we need to approach it again.

Othery cope

> And there appeared a great wonder in heaven: a woman clothed with the sun, and the moon under her feet, and upon her head a crown of twelve stars
> (Revelations 12:1)

Who's that a-sewing?
Ann the restorator
What's she a-sewing?
Ask the restorator
A cope of the (indecipherable) sun

She was clothed with cords
and t ties
twisting out the sweating
minor volcanic
in the sewers of the ruins
the daughter-house
of the rere dorter
harebells in the runis

Who's that a-sewing?
Ann the restorator
What's she a-sewing?
Ask the restorator
A cloak of the (indecipherable) son

She was clothed with the sun
Mary the Virgin, Mary the engine
Origin and trenchant
More guy ses than sh°ines

she is the plasmic   centre stitches a-bursting
closed with the one   pome
            granate

Who made the patches?

Who defines　　　　_____　　　　　　the outlines?

Ann the restorator
Split between cope and car

2

Window through window
Push over Dis/
Solution
In the blue sky Scriptorum

Lady Justice said to me
She said, Christine
Tell me the truth
She said Tell me the truth

Show me the City
Show me the City
Of Ladies that you've built

Then Lady Justice
Led the Queen of Heaven
Into the highest tower
To greet all of us

She is clothed with a book
leaves dangling from her ear lobes
doubling her chin
folding on her belly
dancing on her navel
tasted with her seeds
pages gripped prehensile
letters on her (indecipherable)
　　　　　　　　　　　scroll

CHORUS

Julian of Norwich

Her cell

swept colour
       brushed through
  the glass lozenges

nail feet
       his prehensile toes
altar cloth creases
       morwyn   mor vane
rillets   hail
       storfold
clustered chrysanthemums
       bench burn mark
burn all benchmarks
       mark this bench

you have to see the trees
               through

into this pause flows

thou art enough
       thou art enough

(we fall against each other in the soft bed)

for Joan Brossa

white lamp
votive lamp
learn to kill the flame

make them carry on
funded through public subscription
give them time
but not enough

you have a crucified body
to see what would really happen
how it comes down through
the individual leaves

search for a simpler language
in the paradox of modernism
another kind of popularity
running up this final pine tree

common ground of our beseeching
beloved in every phrase
there's more tea if you want it

first flame

first taper
        candle
                flame

twenty pense
                pence
tapers quenched
per que
tap when

battering ram
at 4 am
was only your breath
and heart beat
too regular
for an armed assault

still leaves
white cyclamen
red hearts
single white flame
snow scarf?
                surf
                      scart
parts
situation/
al
anal
y
sis
sit
you
nations

shimmer
the tiles
'at nine o'clock'

her double flame
ascending
in my head

upend the small red
plastic container
palette
over the flame
mouthing
no reconnaissance

Notes

And on the ground, which is my moodres gate,
I knokke with my staf, bothe erly and late,
And say, 'leeve mooder, leet me in'
        Chaucer *The Pardoner's Tale*

Garrigill, Cumbria, is the home of poet and naturalist Colin Simms, whose works include *Hen Harrier Poems*, published by Shearsman Books, 2015.

Tertia Longmire gave a performance at the close of the exhibition *Apparitions* at St Mary Magdalene church in London, 28 June 2002.

Fluid Canvas, choreographed by Merce Cunningham, performed at the Barbican 11/9/02

Othery Cope is an exploded blues, inspired by *John the Revelator*, sung by Blind Willie Johnson and his wife Angeline. The Othery Cope hangs in the Glastonbury Abbey museum, and was restored by Ann French. I also quote from *The Book of the City of Ladies* by Christine de Pizan.

UNCOLLECT

Conductor

dip rip rhythm

green spills
                (green spirits)
green spits

blank out quotes
blank out quarters
              questers

light masks
      light marks

thumb girder
thumb girdin
thumb guides
      open pages just
open walls almost
open wells

green linesstretch down

chere   phase   4eme
chase these thoughts down

arched windows
crushed felt

strip stip the rock music
      for consolation
skip   slip

only the g^~

fine lines get light to guide
                lost in my eyes

the   not of the   ment
          movement is   move

The Landscape Room

place avenues of trees where none exist

builders, don't build anything

throw a camouflage net of leaves

disappointingly 2D

but you have to stop the children falling in

the grass and lake captioned by nets

smooth	land	slopes
leaves	beautiful	land
slopes	leaves	smooth

: Edmund Burke, who could not be friends

in a revolution

we can still be friends and fractals will give us
that approximation

in this version our view of the landscape
is restricted by a high wire fence
which is unannounced
and prevents any further access

there are still people who come on foot
but they may not walk up the main drive

we are fenced dear
and must lie fallow
watching the deer at a safe distance

this is more like the world as we know it

who has deleted their planting holes?

say the word wild
or a similar word
or a similar

K   T
              E
N   T
                                        T

projection of giant shears from the school bus
planed the hedges
while giant blades mowed the verges

smooth hedges
smooth regulation verges

on vapoured glass
I won at noughts and crosses
by   capturing
          the centre

                    a wicked witch
who cheats at geometry

permitted to enter a copse
in between shots
we're from the world wildlife

prints do not show her geometric fingers
in pointed prayer

long finger shadows crunch sheep shit and clover

or the underlying code that generates

your code				between my

							coast

Huboub

Trimardeur, translated as *Vagabond*, was unfinished at her sudden death in a flash flood at Ain Sefra in October 1904
This is all I can remember about IsAbelle Eberhardt
He had no place amongst men, for he could only ever be either their victim or executioner
She exchanged letters with her brother in which he described his life in the Foreign Legion
The hubBub was caused if at all by the careful packaging of the unfinished
S/he fell in love with an Arab and crossed the line my friends would tell me of
Had not the old man come in with a WhOo-bub against his Daughter and the King's son
This is not a book about escaping into the desert and there is no perfect description of the sanD or the prickly pears

"vagabond" is a more romantic title than "trimardeur" or tramp

vagrant
wave into the flash
no place

        N   O

V   D   B

      A   A

        G

victim trimmer wrote hush entwine next blinded only nascent

over and over donor gaining undine versus oval notion delete

sand storm   (W) H O O P S

A comedy for Colette

> 'some passages were perhaps given in echo, some simultaneously, some spoken as ordinary dialogue, some slow, some fast' COMMEDIA DELL'ARTE

each poach
pass   pass
trespass

                                                      she can sew
                                                         cooed
                                                       cousined

we eat
cooked
wheat

                                                     grain head
                                                        strong
                                                  tatached to
                                          what is in the head

savouring   sand
salient   sale
the salt of the language
she is the salt on her arms
no one can taste

```
                              dry field
                                  fold
              felt near          press
                                   for
                             and against
```

hold your coast
between my
this is the coast of France

your code
between my

his spiny homage
man   age   to   send

she had never known respectful
flattery

Windcorner

                        near St Hildegard's abbey

In Moment
in the moment's process
scrape

white butterfly black dots
dat   dhat   da

rummage scabious
purple clover
hemming by summerhouses

all night
an undercurrent
of bells
overcurrent of birds

I'm going inside my body
sometimes there's nothing
but Genglisch
the gentle pressure of an entire landscape
on the left of my head
it's clearing
yolky

the river moves its houses
for and against
ingenious metaphor

                    a bird of prey
                       flies up
                　 between the vines
              we are flying towards each other

                              this is the head
these are the wings   she was thinking of

           the wings in her drawing
                                        – the ardour of God

Afterthought on 'The ardour of God'

When I met the bird of prey between the vines, on the slope near Hildegard of Bingen's abbey, I immediately thought of the mediaeval illumination of Hildegard's vision: the ardour of God. The title also reminds me of Hopkins' phrase, 'the grandeur of God', and this bird was as powerful as Hopkins' falcon, the 'windhover'. Yet when I look again at Hildegard's text, rather than the image, I find something else, something more terrifying and much darker than anything in Hopkins: the product of a more punitive theology and feudal order. I have used the word 'ardour' when a closer translation might be 'zeal' – this is a zealous God. The ardour or zeal of God forms part of Hildegard's extended vision of the vast 'holy building', which she describes in obsessive detail, using the language of geometry and architecture; but it is also a language of excess and redundancies, in the manner of visions. The zeal of God is identified by a giant human (male) head, with three massive wings, which, however, move less like a bird than a giant machine. These wings are like the vanes on a windmill or propeller, a machine calculated to inflict maximum shock and awe.

'Then I suddenly saw appear, as at the north corner … something like a strangely formed head. Motionless it rests on its neck at the corner of the walls; it was as wide above the earth as the walls were high, it didn't rise above the walls but was as high. And this head was fire red and blazed like a flame. It had an awful human face and looked very angrily to the north. From the neck down I saw no more of this being, because the rest of its body was quite concealed and covered by the wall edge. I only saw the head in the form of a bared male head. It was covered neither in a man's style of hair, nor in a woman's veil, but yet was more male than female and terrible to see.

However, it possessed three wings of astonishing width and length. They were white like a light cloud and did not point upwards. One was stretched out horizontally and the head rose a little above it. The first wing stretched out from the right cheek to the northeast, but the second, which was also the middle one, went from the throat also to the north; the third stretched from the left cheek to the west. At times they began to move in a terrible frightening way and swung round; at times everyone heard them start to turn. I did not hear this head utter any word; it remained motionless and turned its wings.'

Notes

Conductor (pp 309-310) is an installation by Jane Prophet "composed of 120 glowing electro-luminescent cables suspended from the ceiling of a boiler house, with water flooding the floor to a depth of 300 mm". It is cold and dark and damp and hard to see anything except the cables which do not illuminate. My poem was written blind, and then later as an attempt to decipher and recreate the scrawl. I was the first and only visitor that morning, but while I was there someone played rock music in another room.

In Jane Prophet's *The Landscape Room* (pp. 311-313) computer simulated landscapes are combined with photographs taken of Holkham Hall's parkland in Norfolk. My text moves between these prints and the (my) parkland of East Anglia. Robert Kett led the rebellion in Norfolk against the enclosure of common land.

Isabelle Eberhardt's novel *Vagabond*, Hogarth, 1988, trans. Annette Kobak, was published in French in 1922, as *Trimardeur*. (pp. 314-315) It is based on Eberhardt's adventurous life in North Africa. *Huboub* is the Arabic word for sandstorm.

MYNE

*This sequence was written between March 2003 and April 2004
in and around Minehead in Somerset.*

March

on North Hill

above Greenaleigh

for Tilla Brading

lower buds
thinking without

Tilla, the tides
the tides
are always too early
or too late
to swallow
words
nowhere to lay them
on the beach

crests cannot
catch up
too many, white, commas
clustering
not spacing

                                                  on the path
                                  white trainers of morning
                                          her morning
                                    of terracotta terrace
                                                  trend

ended heather
pressure
deeper blue
grounds
sea cloud
say it's dolphins

                                          back pack
                                             voices
                                         remind me
                                         of reading
                                        Martin Eden
                                       on this knoll
                                     disintegrating
                                 edition and waiting
                                      for stragglers

or another burden

this great burden
on my back
will sink me
will sink me lower

these arms around my shoulders
these legs around my waist
between us
we carried
the twins

this great burden ... from John Bunyan's 'Pilgrim's Progress'

in St Michael's

mama you've bin
musical
mu
sicale

ring chan
delire
ban Delilah
my chant delier
is dead

she says
breathing helps
just the body
cycles

hard to tell
that carving is
Michael weighing souls
with so much wear and tear

the inter clock
tock   (tick)   tock   (tick)

we saw
                              u
pulls hymn lines together

what are
twentieth century hymns?

a passage of
air
the upstretch
eagle neck
lectern

April

from Greenaleigh to Porlock Bay
Friday. Good

these black shards
scattered on the field
where sheep and walkers go

piecing together
piece work

**Republic
Ch Republic**

Czech Republic

**Or
nets?
Ar
nets?**

Hornets

black saucers
must be clay pigeons
tap they
clay
not plastic

come blow your horn

*

remembering semtex
the shifting sense
the shifting S

*

Site of Special Scientific Interest
see today
sea pitched
sea level
subsequent storms

the new salt marsh
no more freshwater
the salt line
grey grass
bleached trees
byre useless

sea birds
come skeeting home

walking back past lambs
he was talking ahead of me
about the Sibylline
lore and the ambiguity of
Sibylline law

June

on North Hill

blind drawing

for Kelvin Corcoran

axial
fear bone
tender acorns
tender engines
probe frames
angular
tri angular
spot sun
is this blind drawing
and where?

warm fingers to lip
tidal surge and resurge
Colette sounds
thunder collect

broken bark
smoothes my face

a branch is forking down the clouds
turning pen into shadowline
and pylon
branches chased to sea

        West, is where you're tending
              he said

how do we survive the westward
surf culture
the fear of immigration
the fear of immigrant self?

not detachment
but embrace
and the interchangeability
of frames

real drawing is like this
and now I have made
the bridge too wide
the peak again
piercing the pubic bone
the public bone
rising

                                        Kelvin said
                                Just the sea, Frances

sur sur sur sur
sur surring

su   su   su   rus

October

on North Hill

bless test
mess of leaves
wings will not make

                                        serious
                                        back pack
                                        stride

fern returns
leaf crisps
clenched
hear
here

break   stop   wave
make it return
a flick of the wrist
she hasn't got
yet

       who has not built
       a house
       will now no longer
       will not build

                                          no nay never
                                          or some version
                                          on the march
                                          against
                                          war

no more
builds now
who has not yet
who has not built
yet builds now
bilds

(this is the dialogue of memory)

bird rattle
sun slats
through dry leaves

like the turning
segments
of glass
at Foreland Point
occulting the optic

                        white outriders

                                  over ride the line

November

in St Michael's

click dot
heavier drop
three dots
              S   .   .   .

O'
Jack
Lantern gone
no shifting
no human shifting

purse
        perse
parse
        prestige
point   counterpoint
steady tick and downbeat
release

sun   sudden   expansion
twist untwist   dazzle
it's coming through
the red
it's open
makes stop
on rotten stump
red breast

As pants the hart
hart stress has been noted
it was never this loud
drags back from my scalp
cooling Streams

December

in St Peter's

wet not stop
soak paper
soak away

too many changes
of tone
break
lose faith
but I know the rhythm
and could have cobbled

                                            barrels scrape
                                                the quay

knee damp
rot behind the altar
blue wall gone brown
wreckage on the floor
fish kneelers

holding this away from wet cuffs
capsize me

s/he stands on the water
not even the hem is wet
in the midst is not
on the water
                          to be in the midst

coal ship
the last
no glowing embers

sea pelt
sea srus
soak away from the last inn

altar cord accord
lower the ceiling
draw in the walls

prion   prevaricates   holding
preheed   paddocks   heaved

February

in St Michael's

the sound of the hoover:
                                             (burrs catches on skin
                                                   furs throat lining
                                                         sounds like
                                                      the line under
                                               the dead straight way)

turn around sound
catches its breath
bones and tiptones
the lining of my throat
the dust still vocal

            above
her hoover   movement
she is hovering
the altar
sun on green carpet

2

he was holding the kettle
above the birdbath
melting the ice

gold tipped wings
and straight back
against the low tree
holding their
(apple)
onyx

such an one and
such an one

beware the bullfinch
flat caps go flatter

3

pull
                                        strike
pull

light lines across
the spiral steps

              no
      admittance

no   trespass

                            step

                                                  across

March

on North Hill

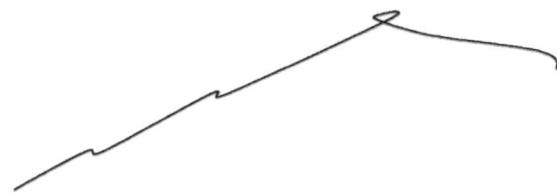

                              Dunkery

intakes
in breaks

oar   oare   or

bromage

between   yellow
high   gorse

                and white
                root strips
                into your tangle

lark calls (?)
       last calls

from
                                                    and to

in St Michael's

lip slide
these women had not
exerted themselves
had not
broken any rings
corseleted
corsle
cors

                                             below the red
                                             Magdalene
                                             a single
                                             dead rosebud
                                             not for Lent
                                             but

                                        | in celebration |
                                        | of a ∿ |
                                        | I never knew |
                                        | (A Daughter) |

in St Peter's

four minutes
out blank
white lines
think in
float

stir boat
how do fish manage
without (?) spires
            without spines
this is the question I asked
but ultimately the story takes over
for pixar

Chris
carries the child on his shoulder
feet in the water

he says that some didn't complain at all
and those who did
should never have gone
to Disneyland

fan still
merchants cross
grey dawn bray   a   aching
I do not want

fables followed
her cast wide
the net

better than
faster than
quay board

April

on Grabbist

for Ian Robinson

saint george traffics
scrub oak bends further

lichen thickens
too many twists
in these trees
the weight of moss
the fracture of bark
sitting bone cracks

'it was that bone which got broken in my neck . . .
the one they break when they hang people'

sand stones
percolate
periculo

black burnt gorse
'too late to save the heather'

they're making a clearance for
the purple headed mountain
because it is written
and according to estate

tree spindles upwards
economically inactive
but greening

circle these iron circles

cypress skyline
teeth towers
dark drawn in
shorthand
fade out

green circles move and tilt
leftward and
rightward slopes

sun on neck
uncircled

these sticks
my arms
will kindle
in gorse flower
air

....
'Thanks for the card — more trees! ... A tree does finally sneak its way in in the last of the enclosed drawings. I do hope you like them all — I meant to do 3 only but I tend to work in series until the vein is exhausted. It isn't quite yet.'
(from Ian Robinson, 3/5/00)

Acknowledgements

This volume contains work previously collected in *Paravane* (2004) and *Myne* (2006), with some additions.

I'm very grateful to Chris Hamilton-Emery of Salt Publishing for permission to reprint material from *Paravane: new and selected poems 1996–2003*.

Some of this work was made with my long-time friends and collaborators: Tilla Brading, Irma Irsara, elizabeth james and Peterjon Skelt.

'Windcorner' & 'Afterthought on "The ardour of God"' originally published in German, translated by Hans Thill: *Der Knabe singts im Wunderhorn* ed. Michael Buselmeier, Verlag, 2006.

www.ingramcontent.com/pod-product-compliance
Lightning Source LLC
Chambersburg PA
CBHW021801220426
43662CB00006B/144